MW01028443

"Dispelling the eco-h
of 'business better ti.
green seem as American as (organic!) apple pie. Read *Green, American Style*, then pass it along to a friend. It will change your life—satisfaction guaranteed."

> Matthew Sleeth, author of *Serve God, Save the Planet*, and Nancy Sleeth, author of *Go Green, Save Green*

"Anna Clark provides a practical guide for those wanting to learn more about minimizing the impact their lives have on our planet, especially as consumers. Clark's insights, drawn from her personal journey to living sustainably, make this book a joy to read."

> Jim Thomas, vice president of corporate social responsibility, JC Penney

"Regardless of our belief system or worldview, we've all asked ourselves, 'What really matters?' and 'How can I make a difference?' Anna Clark asked herself these questions and took action, embarking on a mission to make the world a better place one step at a time. She invites us into the conversations she's having with green leaders and friends across America who are seeking a greener way of living that saves money, our health, and our planet. At a time when many of us are experiencing 'green fatigue,' *Green, American Style* inspires us to think smarter, cultivate natural-grown leadership skills in others and ourselves, and use our pioneering spirit to cause a ripple effect that will transform our communities, our country, and our world."

> Lee Enry Erickson, community manager for SustainLane Creation, www.sustainlane.com/creation-care

"In *Green, American Style*, Anna Clark takes the outsized and overwhelming world of sustainable living—from the living room to the corporate boardroom—and turns it into an engaging and detailed look at the green economy that's rapidly taking root across the country. Through extensive interviews with green leaders ranging from oil tycoons to suburban chicken farmers, *Green, American Style* makes the case that every individual and every business can play a part in and benefit from the greening of America."

Matthew Wheeland, managing editor of GreenBiz.com

"Well done, Anna! The more those of us who are helping our planet recover from the ravages to which we have subjected it are made to seem normal and correct, the more 'Joe and Josephine Citizen' will be inclined to do their bit without thinking that they're behaving on the fringes. This is a book everyone should read!"

Tony Frost, former head of the World Wildlife Foundation in South Africa; author of *After the Rain*

GREEN,
American Style

**Becoming Earth-Friendly
and Reaping the Benefits**

Anna M. Clark

BakerBooks
a division of Baker Publishing Group
Grand Rapids, Michigan

Published by Baker Books
a division of Baker Publishing Group
P.O. Box 6287, Grand Rapids, MI 49516-6287
www.bakerbooks.com

Printed in the United States of America

Library of Congress Cataloging-in-Publication Data
Clark, Anna M., 1973–
    Green, American style : becoming earth-friendly and reaping the benefits /
Anna M. Clark.
        p.   cm.
    Includes bibliographical references.
    ISBN 978-0-8010-1334-8 (pbk.)
    1. Green movement—United States. 2. Human ecology—United States.
3. Environmentalism—United States. 4. Sustainable living—United States.
I. Title.
GE197.C43 2010
304.2′8—dc22   2009046922

Unless otherwise indicated, Scripture is taken from the HOLY BIBLE, NEW INTER-NATIONAL VERSION®. NIV®. Copyright © 1973, 1978, 1984 by International Bible Society. Used by permission of Zondervan. All rights reserved.

Scripture marked NLT is taken from the *Holy Bible*, New Living Translation, copyright © 1996, 2004. Used by permission of Tyndale House Publishers, Inc., Wheaton, Illinois 60189. All rights reserved.

Excerpt from "Strong Men" in *The Book of American Negro Poetry*, edited by James Weldon Johnson, copyright 1931, 1922 by Houghton Mifflin Harcourt Publishing Company and renewed 1959, 1950 by Mrs. Grace Nail Johnson, reprinted by permission of the publisher.

10   11   12   13   14   15   16   7   6   5   4   3   2   1

For my beautiful children Jordan and Ryan, my two favorite reasons for doing this work. For my beloved husband Michael, my rock. For my father who inspired me to write. For my mother, my constant encourager.

And for God, who makes it all possible.

Contents

Acknowledgments   9
Introduction   11

Part 1: The Next American Revolution
1. Eco-Mania: The Truth behind the Hype   19
2. The Roots of a Green Revolution   31
3. The Rise of Eco-Capitalism   59
4. God's Green Soldiers   83

Part 2: 85 Easy Ways to Save the Planet (and Money!)
5. A Starter's Guide to Greener Living   103
6. Organic Cuisine, Sustainable Wine, and Local Flavor   123
7. Eco-Chic Cars, Clothes, and Other Essentials   143
8. A Buyer's Guide to Toxin-Free Living   161
9. Blueprint for a Green Remodel   177
10. Urban Oasis or Sustainable Suburb?   193
11. Green Games Your Kids Will Love   209

Part 3: Being the Change

12. Green at Work   219
13. Finding Your Voice   233

    Discussion Questions   243
    Notes   247

Acknowledgments

Writing this book is my latest step on a journey that began in 2005 with the founding of my company, EarthPeople. So many names deserve mention, but I would like to extend special thanks and recognition to the following people:

Chrissy Runyan, Dan Weisenbach, and Terry Gips for lending me your wisdom, support, and expertise when I needed it most.

Betsy Healy for leading me to my first client, Cannon Flowers.

Cindy Bishop and Kevin Colbert for hiring EarthPeople for our first full sustainability engagement.

Nancy Lovell for teaching me to write.

Matt Wheeland and the editors at Greenbiz.com for being the first to give me a platform for writing.

Lee Enry Erickson, creation care manager at SustainLane .com, for helping me extend my green mission beyond the business community.

Christine Cashen, an amazing mentor and dynamic professional speaker.

Tim Durkin, an incredible motivator.

Pat Gibbons, an inspiration.

Ann Drumm and the Dallas Sierra Club for introducing me to the world of activism.

Dr. Matthew and Nancy Sleeth for sharing their life-changing message with me, and Margie Haley, who first brought them to Dallas.

My wonderful literary agent Rachelle Gardner for believing in me, and acquisitions editor Chad Allen for seeing my vision.

Bobbi Jo Heyboer, Jessica Miles, Adam Ferguson, Brooke Nolen, and the other staff at Baker for their support and guidance.

Debora Annino, Scott Arves, Carey Bradley, Jon and Ashleigh Bull, Stefane Burress, Rod and Julie Dreher, Blake and Dulcey Fulenwider, Mike Gill, Lee Hall, Gail Haterius, Lisa Heisinger, Alan and Pam Hoffmann, Michael Honig, Deirdre Imus, Bryan Korba, Bruce Leadbetter, Dale Long, Doug Newton, T. Boone Pickens, Kim Rice, Craig Senglin, Beth Shumate, Henry Sullivan, Jim Thomas, Philip Williams, and others who lent their knowledge and stories to this book.

My friends and family for your encouragement, especially my sister Amy, my mother Jeanne, my father Allen, my mother-in-law Mary Louise, and my wonderful husband Michael. And special thanks to Granny for all her love and support. You are all so dear to me.

Introduction

I t began as an experiment. What would it be like if I tried living life from a completely new angle? I had my reasons for going this direction, some voluntary, others not so much. But during the course of this transition, I discovered something amazing. Living greener is a better way to live. It's easy. It's exciting. It's convenient. It's purposeful. It's fruitful. It's fun. It's none of the things I thought. I thought it would be about giving up, but I ended up saving money, getting healthy, finding my voice, making money, making a difference, and taking life at a more enjoyable pace. When I decided to take a break from living "luxuriously," I finally learned how to live well. The secret? Sustainability, or what I like to call the "green advantage."

The green advantage has worked so well for me that I can't help but share my enthusiasm with anyone who will listen, so I started a consulting firm that would allow me to do just that. My company, EarthPeople, visits organizations large and small with the aim of teaching them how to be more profitable through eco-friendly practices. The goal is sustainability, which has been defined as "meeting the needs of the present without compromising the ability of future generations to meet their own needs."[1]

In my experience, too many people still think sustainability is nonsense. The green movement has become so politicized that it's easy to forget that it started as a necessary reaction to industrial threats to our human health and natural resources. Long before Al Gore took center stage, there were Americans in every generation (including presidents) who championed the cause of conservation. Even if the climate-change debate rages for decades, our individual beliefs about it have little bearing on the good we can do by practicing commonsense sustainability.

That said, it's just human nature to resist change. I mean, why would I want to grow my own tomatoes when the store is just down the street? Besides, isn't my time too valuable to grow tomatoes? And change the lightbulbs? Is it really worth it?

In the summer of 2008, the price of oil hit an all-time high, breaking the historical record. The cost of energy soared. Then a national outbreak of salmonella infested our tomatoes. Hmmm . . . maybe green living makes sense after all.

We still need to accept some cold realities. Americans represent 5 percent of the world's population, and we consume 30 percent of the world's resources. If you think that's impossible, consider one example: cell phones. Americans dispose of 426,000 of them every day. Few are recycled. And then there are plastic bags. The average American uses 18,306 shopping bags in a lifetime. We use them for an average of just 30 minutes apiece, but each plastic bag takes 1,000 years to decompose. Americans throw out 18 billion disposable diapers each year—enough to stretch around the world 90 times. That's part of the reason an American at age one already has a bigger carbon footprint than a Tanzanian will in a lifetime.[2]

Our hyperconsumption is not limited to consumer goods. Overconsumption even extends to natural resources on which life depends: air, water, land, and sea. Until now, most of us have taken for granted that the earth's resources are renewable, but not at the rate we are consuming them. The unique thing about America is that with so much abundance around us, we cannot imagine how our consumption affects others less fortunate than we are. We have no idea that one in five people in the world survives on less water per day than is used to flush a toilet. We have no idea that every day, more than 16,000 children die from hunger-related causes. This is one child every five seconds.[3]

As we begin to overtax the earth's resources, the natural balance of things is being thrown out of whack. Already, over 800 million people suffer from hunger and malnutrition. Infertility and asthma rates are approaching epidemic proportions. We can argue that these conditions, taken separately, stem from a range of factors. But from an ecological perspective, they are inextricably linked.

How many of us have a deep or even shallow understanding of ecology? I have a university education and can remember learning about ecology only for a few weeks here and there— as a youngster in science camp or while cramming for a biology test. No wonder so many of us are in denial about the crisis occurring in our natural world.

While years of speculation and suspicion around sustainability have given way to a certainty among some, the rest of us remain stuck in inertia and irritation. We have eco-facts, eco-checklists, eco-this, and eco-that coming through every crevice of the airwaves. This is giving us eco-fatigue. We have plenty of experts telling us what to do; what we still lack is the will to do it. This rigid mind-set is the single greatest barrier to financial progress for companies and healthy lifestyle choices for individuals in a changing world.

Just how rapidly is the world changing? Twenty-five years ago most folks didn't own personal computers, and fifteen years ago the internet had only just begun to take off. Today people are walking around with computers in their pockets, and anyone on the globe can connect with anyone else instantaneously via the world wide web. Ray Kurzweil's law of accelerating returns tells us that in the twenty-first century, we will experience not one hundred years of progress—more like twenty thousand years of progress. We are now squarely in the information age. Knowledge about subjects once considered esoteric is becoming commonplace. People's expectations about what to eat, what to buy, where to live, what to do, and where to shop are rising. The effects have been good for quality of life in the short term, but not so great for the health of the planet—and us—in the long term. How do we balance that? It's the million-dollar question.

I was sitting on the plane today, ready to dive into my writing and secretly hoping the lady next to me wouldn't try to make conversation. But I gave in because I was curious about her accent. It turned out she was from Mexico City. From the first few sentences she spoke, I could tell she was highly educated. She was in her seventies, so listening to her was like hearing a firsthand account of twentieth-century Mexican history. In the span of an hour, we spoke about the Mexican Revolution, globalization, the explosion of rampant consumerism, the disparity between rich and poor, and political corruption. I was struck by the sameness of the issues occurring in countries all over the world.

"Do you know how lucky you are?" she said to me. "America is a great country; there is nothing else like it."

I was astonished. Usually after discussing social ills on a global scale, particularly with a foreigner, the conversation turns to why it's America's fault.

"Wow, you mean you don't resent us?" I asked.

"Oh, never," she exclaimed. "I respect and admire the people of your country. My country almost seems beyond help. America is utterly unique. Your system is based on more than a single leader. You have a real democracy. And you seem to work very hard."

She's right. We do live in a great country. We Americans are ever industrious, not to mention creative and innovative. What we have created really is remarkable.

But here's the thing: we could lose it. History shows what happens when cultures lose sight of the values that got them where they are. Before ancient Rome succumbed to ruin and France to revolution, they represented several of the most affluent, educated, and accomplished cultures in history. Too much of a good thing can poison the moral fiber of a society in the same way that water intoxication can drown the body. We have lived in abundance for so long that most of us have lost perspective at best and been spoiled at worst. If you want to know the state of our culture today, just turn on your TV. Eight hundred channels and nothing decent to watch. Enough said?

It's time to end the debate and get into action. Being a laggard is not the American way. By embracing commonsense practices such as energy efficiency and conservation, as well as new technologies and different ways of doing things, we can still maintain a high standard of living while enjoying the benefits of cleaner air, healthier foods, new markets for workers and investors, and more time with our friends, families, and neighbors. Green is patriotic. It's the new red, white, and blue. Going green isn't about giving up. In fact, it may be our best chance to preserve our way of life for the future.

I did not begin this journey as a sustainability expert. I began as a citizen, a mom, and a neighbor taking tiny steps forward in the only ways I knew how. I began to recycle. I asked my mother to join me in walking my neighborhood to drop off letters asking others to recycle too. I joined the local Sierra Club, America's largest and oldest environmental organization. I started to learn. I wrote letters to my elected officials. I funneled everything I was learning about sustainability principles into a consulting practice to help others.

While the process did not unfold seamlessly, I found inspiration in Thomas Edison's words: "If we all did the things we are capable of doing, we would literally astound ourselves." Edison showed us the value of persistence when he said, "I have not failed. I've just found 10,000 ways that won't work." Who knows what we can accomplish when we learn to take a few calculated risks to test our ideas? When the payoff can be a better, cleaner world, what do we have to lose by trying?

Being green isn't about being perfect. It's about being a little bit better one step at a time until you look up and discover you've reached new heights and you're taking others with you. I know because that is exactly what I've been doing for the past five years. When I first got into green living, I thought there were only a few places where it mattered in my life. The more you read, the more you'll appreciate how few places there are where green doesn't apply.

My purpose in writing this book is to share easy, flexible, and practical green-living principles that will inspire you to become more planet-friendly in every aspect of your daily life. I invite you to find ways to integrate these principles into your lifestyle in whatever manner makes sense for you. I think the topics covered will be of interest to most readers, but since everyone is in a different place on the green journey, feel free to skip around to the areas that interest you the most. For example, if you have already mastered organic gardening, try working on the many other ways to lighten your environmental load. At the end of this book are discussion questions to share with your friends.

Whatever you get out of reading will be magnified tenfold when you begin to talk it through with other people. In fact, that's the best part. Green living connects you with people in ways you can't imagine. You'll build community, forge alliances, gain influence, and make a difference as others join your mission. The green advantage can make you and yours healthier and happier. It can even be a path to spiritual renewal and a way to honor God's creation.

I know all this enthusiasm may come off as a sales pitch, but it's not. It's a promise. While looking for a reasonable way to make a difference, I stumbled onto the opportunity of a lifetime. Let me tell you about the things I've seen since trading in my rose-colored glasses for green ones.

PART 1

The Next American Revolution

1

Eco-Mania: The Truth behind the Hype

[Global warming is] the greatest hoax ever
perpetrated on the American people.

James Inhofe, US Senator

[Clean technology] is bigger than the Internet, I think by an order of magnitude.

John Doerr, venture capitalist

Are you sick and tired of reading green-related hype
every time you turn on the TV or open the newspaper?
Every day the headlines reveal new catastrophes: "Oil Sky-
rockets to $130 a Barrel." "Climate Change Threatens New
Dust Bowl." "Are All the Frogs Disappearing?" If all this
eco-mania is giving you eco-fatigue, you're not alone.

To the layperson, the green phenomenon must seem like
endless jockeying between the liberal media "pushing their
agenda" and the conservatives lashing back with "fear tactics"

and "junk science." One has to wonder, "Aren't there any moderate, independent thinkers left?" If you are reading this book, I believe you must be one of them—and our country needs your voice now more than ever.

America has been mired in political divisiveness for too long. Green is the glue that can bring us back together. This secret— that green is, in fact, *good*—is coming out in boardrooms, schoolrooms, and living rooms across America. But for many others, the secret still remains under wraps. There is so much to learn, so much to teach, and still not enough teachers. It will be up to people like you and me to show everyone else the way forward. It's a responsibility, but it's also an opportunity.

The American Way

If we could shrink the earth's population to a village of 100 people, with all existing human ratios remaining the same, it would look something like this:

- 61 would be Asian
- 13 would be African
- 12 would be European
- 14 would be from the Western Hemisphere
- 31 would be Christians
- 69 would be non-Christians
- 18 would be illiterate
- 25 would not have shelter from the wind and rain
- 1 would be dying of starvation
- 17 would be undernourished
- 17 would have no clean, safe water to drink
- 8 would speak English
- 1 would have a college education
- 1 would own a computer[1]

The world looks lopsided, if not dismal, for one-quarter of the globe, and opportunity is vastly limited for many others. Americans (only 5 percent of the world's population) live in a land of privilege and wealth beyond imagination. Yet, although we appear to be the lucky winners in the lottery of life, I wonder if life offers more enduring prizes than material abundance. Could it be that all those other people who seem so unlike us know something about life we don't?

America may be the world's most prosperous nation, but for 99 percent of us, that doesn't equate to a life of leisure. Even though we enjoy the highest standard of living in the world, we still aren't the happiest people. In fact, at number 16, the United States ranks below 15 other countries in happiness levels, according to the World Values Survey data in the journal *Perspectives on Psychological Science*. Denmark came in at number 1.

> *Who is rich?*
> *He that is content.*
> *Who is that? Nobody.*
>
> Benjamin Franklin, founding father, political satirist, and inventor

Most of us work so hard that we are too tired to come home and cook a meal. It's no wonder 50 percent of our food dollars are spent on fast food. Given our fast-food addiction, the rate of Americans classified as overweight has risen to a shocking 65 percent. Approximately 127 million people age 20 or older are overweight, and one-third of these are obese, according to the American Obesity Association.[2] "If these trends continue," explains Youfa Wang, an associate professor with Johns Hopkins Bloomberg School of Public Health, "more than 86 percent of adults will be overweight or obese by 2030."[3]

And as hard as we work, we are not necessarily getting ahead. Almost half of American families spend more than they earn each year. Personal bankruptcies doubled in a single decade, from 1993 to 2003, according to the American Bankruptcy Institute. Even after the laws were restructured to discourage bankruptcy, personal bankruptcy filings continue to come near or reach the one-million mark each year.

If everyone in the world lived like the average American, we would need three to five planets to sustain us.[4] Problem: we have only one planet. It boggles the mind to think what will happen when we begin running low on water to drink, oil to burn, land to plow, and clean air to breathe. Will we still have enough of our social fiber intact to weather that storm? There has to be a better way to live.

Lessons We Forgot to Learn

My wise father often admonishes me, "Angel, you don't know your history. You need to read *The Decline and Fall of the Roman Empire*. You need to read *Plutarch's Lives*. Knowing your history will guarantee that you don't have to do time on the couch. It will give you perspective."

No matter how problematic our collective loss of perspective is, finding time for the likes of Will Durant and Edward Gibbon is beyond challenging. I have a household and a family to tend to and a business to run. On top of that, there is the internet to surf, the blogosphere to read, HBO to watch, and two email accounts to check every day. With such a plethora of gadgetry making demands on my time 24-7—under the guise of serving my critical entertainment and information-seeking needs—reading history seems so, well, passé.

But after spending so much time in the green scene, even I can end up with a bad case of eco-fatigue, and nothing takes me away from it all better than a good book. As I write this, I just finished crying my eyes out over *Gone with the Wind*, one of my all-time favorites. After reflecting on this book, I recognized in its emphasis on luxurious living an important parallel between today's American culture and that of the Old South. And in its emphasis on community, I also realized how far we have strayed from our roots.

Remarkably, I opened the book in order to escape an unstable world, only to be thrust into another one. I was soon caught up in the lives of the characters and moved by the intensity of their circumstances. Comparing it with today's climate of individualism, relative peace, and political apathy, I am humbled by the bravery that led Civil War soldiers on both sides to fight to the death to preserve their vision of what America should become. I was thunderstruck by the beauty, and the notable lack of political correctness, in Margaret Mitchell's words as she described the antebellum South:

> They topped the rise and the white house reared its perfect symmetry before her, tall of columns, wide of verandas, flat of roof, beautiful as a woman is beautiful who is so sure of her charm that she can be generous and gracious to all. Scarlett loved Twelve Oaks even more than Tara, for it had a stately beauty, a mellowed dignity that Gerald's house did not possess.
>
> The wide curving driveway was full of saddle horses and carriages and guests alighting and calling greetings to friends. Grinning negroes, excited as always at a party, were leading the animals to the barnyard to be unharnessed and unsaddled for the day. Swarms of children, black and white, ran yelling about the newly green lawn, playing hopscotch and tag and boasting how much they were going to eat. The wide hall which ran from front to back of the house was swarming with people, and as the O'Hara carriage drew up at the front steps, Scarlett saw girls in crinolines, bright as butterflies, going up and coming down the stairs from the second floor, arms about each other's waists, stopping to lean over the delicate handrail of the banisters, laughing and calling to young men in the hall below them.[5]

Through Mitchell's superb characterization, I witnessed the unraveling and Reconstruction of the Old South with emotion tinged with sadness. I was transported to a time where the tightly rooted network of family and neighbors went generations deep, with love of land and country binding them and seeing them through unfathomable privations.

Swinging wildly away from my usual egalitarian hyperbole, I daydreamed about dressing up and being waited on by servants. How grand life must have been as a belle!

This romantic tableau of the Old South is broken only when I remind myself of its harsh underbelly: it was built on slave labor and favored the rich plantation owners. At the same time Margaret Mitchell was writing *Gone with the Wind*, a black Yale professor named Sterling Brown penned his own view of the Old South from a slave's perspective in his 1931 poem "Strong Men." Just reading a few lines was like having a cold bucket of water dumped over my head:

> They dragged you from homeland,
> They chained you in coffles,
> They huddled you spoon-fashion in filthy hatches,
> They sold you to give a few gentlemen ease.
> They broke you in like oxen,
> They scourged you,
> They branded you,
> They made your women breeders,
> They swelled your numbers with bastards. . . .
> They taught you the religion they disgraced.[6]

Brown's eloquence brings to life the horrible realities of slavery. Just imagine, while Scarlett and her friends were living the high life, those who served them were torn from their families, broken like wild animals, beaten, branded, forced to breed and bear their children in hovels, and abandoned to a life of hard labor and servitude. It sounds like hell on earth to me. Reading this poem broke my reverie of nostalgia for the Old South. I still cherish *Gone with the Wind* for its timeless beauty and artful, if idealized, depiction of a bygone era, but I feel wiser for having read both sides. I am closer to understanding the truth of the times than if I had read just one.

How often do we try to see from a different point of view? Most of the time we just go along with whatever affirms our own worldview, never questioning its validity or fairness. How often do we stop to think of who is making the sacrifice for us to live so large? Maybe we don't because it's too painful. As Scarlett O'Hara used to say, "I won't think about that now, I'll die if I do. I'll think about that tomorrow."[7]

Could that be what's wrong with our country today? We as voters, as shareholders, as citizens, and as consumers want immediate returns without sacrifice. When it comes time to make the hard choices to give up for the greater good, we choose the easy way out. And we can only blame our politicians so much. We are their constituents. They are a reflection of us.

> *It is difficult to get a man to understand something when his salary depends upon his not understanding it.*
>
> Upton Sinclair, Pulitzer Prize–winning author

What happened to us in the last 150 years? My guess is that technology and material comfort have sapped us of some of our survival instincts. Not enough of us have retained the fierce patriotism and pioneering spirit of our ancestors.

Technology and globalization are a given. The genie is out of the bottle, and there is no going back. Sometimes the only way to preserve the present is by yielding a bit to the future. The best thing we can do to manage change is to revisit some of our lost traditions and, in other cases, establish new ones. We need to tighten the familial and community bonds that are the fabric of our culture, but seek flexible, creative, and innovative ways of doing it. The Old South died under its unwillingness to adapt to a new world. Ultimately, it was more important that America remain intact than for one faction to cling to its ways. That is a lesson we would be foolish to forget.

Citizens in Cultural Change

Some will always remain steadfast in their position in the face of overwhelming evidence to the contrary. So if enough evidence is in to support an immediate and widespread green movement, why does the debate go on? There is no easy answer. Some are spreading confusion on purpose, others because they don't understand. Some are motivated by fear, others by greed. Some resist change in order to maintain their position. And many others are just plain unmotivated.

Alan AtKisson, a leading sustainability expert, developed a model that illustrates citizens' roles in cultural change. He uses a giant amoeba as a symbol of our culture. The amoeba is a single-celled animal that creeps along by sticking out a pseudopod (foot) into new territory. In human society, the pseudopod is the domain of "innovators," people rarely happy with the status quo. They exert their creative energies in devising solutions to societal problems.[8]

> *The vast majority of human beings dislike and even actually dread all notions with which they are not familiar. . . . Hence it comes about that at their first appearance innovators have generally been persecuted, and always derided as fools and madmen.*
>
> Aldous Huxley, English
> novelist and poet

The bulk of people represented in the amoeba are "mainstreamers" who tend to see things as okay just the way they are. "Laggards" are located at the tail end of the mainstream and are particularly complacent. The "reactionaries" actively resist change because it threatens their vested interest (for example, a products manufacturer covering up scientific findings on the danger of the chemicals used to manufacture their products).

Real change happens when the mainstream's "transformers," flexible people with a tendency toward curiosity, respond to reasonable arguments and act on concrete suggestions. It is the job of the "change agents" to build the bridge for the "transformers" to cross, thereby dragging forward the entire amoeba.

The Anatomy of Cultural Change

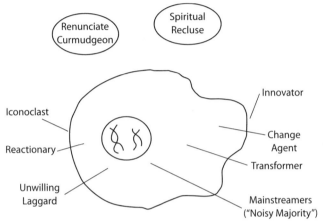

Illustration excerpted from "The Innovation Diffusion Game" by Alan AtKisson, reprinted by permission from In Context #28—Making It Happen, Spring 1991, copyright © 1991, 1996 by Context Institute, www.context.org.

The amoeba of social transformation is not universally applicable to everyone all the time. We may be laggards and reactionaries in some areas and transformers and change agents in others. In the case of the green movement, anyone who applies the green advantage will have the power to transform our culture for the better. Some might even produce new innovations for others to follow. But before that can happen, more of us must learn how to think for ourselves.

The Media: The Fourth Branch of Government

"Is Google Making Us Stoopid?" Nicholas Carr, who wrote this cover story for the July/August 2008 issue of *Atlantic Monthly*, thinks so. Eighty years ago Franklin Delano

Roosevelt would hold "fireside chats" over the radio, explaining to listeners in great detail his plans to end World War II. Today most of us don't have time to watch the evening news, let alone sit down as a family to discuss the finer points of public policy.

For anyone who followed O. J. Simpson's trial, who could forget the success of the late Johnny Cochran's phrase, "If it does not fit, you must acquit"? While many of us laughed at the apparent stupidity of the jurors, the record shows how susceptible we are to sound bites. Consequently, we know a little about a lot, but when it comes to the complex, we don't have a clue. This phenomenon has been dubbed "the dumbing down of America."

A good newspaper, I suppose, is a nation talking to itself.

Arthur Miller, playwright
and essayist

Much of the confusion surrounding eco-mania can be attributed to the media's role in perpetuating the argument about global warming. However, since the media tends to spoon-feed us what we want to hear, we are partially to blame. Although we have always had freedom of speech, public discourse used to occur in a shared forum. The same books and newspapers were widely read by everyone.

Today, we draw news from biased, highly fragmented blogs, websites, videos, discussion groups, and hundreds of satellite TV and radio channels. We are so easily distracted that few of us are likely to get the full story. Every time I check my email, I'm pulled in by the headlines that flash on the screen, but after I read a couple lines, I'm on to the next. It is exhausting.

I remember a class being offered in college that looked fascinating: "The Media: The Fourth Branch of Government." Think how our world has changed since the framers of the Constitution so brilliantly drafted that document. They conceived a delicate system of checks and balances to carefully and evenly distribute power among three branches of government: legislative, executive, and judicial. But if the media shapes public opinion, a fourth group is also in power: the journalists. And here's the interesting twist—there is no means to keep the power of the media in check because it is defended by the First Amendment, freedom of speech.

The Declaration of Independence says that all men are created equal. Amen to that. However, while the media may give equal weight to differing opinions, can we really conclude that all *opinions* are created equal? Are some opinions as informed as others? Albert Einstein said, "I never bother to remember anything I can look up," which was his way of saying he was willing to leave the thinking up to someone else at least some of the time. But even Einstein—especially Einstein—was judicious in the resources he chose to trust. If you are still reading, I believe you are too. And the world needs thoughtful people like you to start taking action.

The green movement is not about taking away a life of privilege for a few so that the many may have freedom. In fact, it's opening up new opportunities for the most privileged to expand their wealth, and it gives the rest of us a chance at new jobs, abundant energy, cleaner air, and the promise of a future for our kids. Going green does not require anyone to sell out or give up long-held values. Green is a train that we can all climb aboard. And like every other time in history when the guard changes, the ones who get a head start are the ones most successful in the new order. As Rhett Butler told Scarlett O'Hara, "There are two times when fortunes are made: when a civilization collapses, and when one begins."[9] But one question still remains: are we in a beginning or a collapse?

2

The Roots of a Green Revolution

Every generation needs a new revolution.

President Thomas Jefferson

Revolution. That sounds grandiose, doesn't it? Not to mention dangerous. We're seeing this word linked to the green movement with increasing frequency. A book by *New York Times* columnist Tom Friedman even uses the word in the title: *Hot, Flat, and Crowded: Why We Need a Green Revolution—and How It Can Renew America.* So, does *revolution* really apply? I'll let you decide that for yourself. What I will say is that revolutions only *appear* to happen overnight, so don't be too quick to discount the possibility for the future without understanding the present. Most people never see revolutions coming. If Marie Antoinette had expected the guillotine, she probably would have done things differently.

As a lay student of history, I've always found revolutionaries intriguing. In every generation a core group of people becomes the earliest architects of a new order. When we think of the American Revolution, for example, a committed group of visionaries inspired men to fight and die for the most basic of human rights: freedom. How can we possibly liken that to the plight of preachy, Birkenstock-wearing, tree-hugging enviros banding together to save obscure species and stop progress? Well, we can't. That's because the stereotype of one faction of the green revolution has a tendency to overshadow the myriad and complex forces that are contributing to the greening of America.

Popular Uprising

A revolution occurs when some aspect of society becomes so unjust that it reaches a tipping point, triggering a swell of people to take action to preserve the rights they hold dear. The goal of the green revolution is difficult to grasp because we have multiple interest groups with different motives mobilizing around what only appears to be the same goal. As a result, anyone who champions an initiative designed to reduce energy use, slow climate change, eliminate toxins from food, clean our water, clean our air, reduce our dependence on foreign oil, help the poor, and save the whales is labeled "green."

Never doubt that a small group of thoughtful, committed citizens can change the world. Indeed, it is the only thing that ever has.

Margaret Mead, writer and anthropologist

The poster child for the green revolution may be your typical environmental activist, but other factions include growing numbers of faith leaders, soccer moms, oil tycoons, Ivy League intellectuals, church ladies, Republican businessmen, and almost everybody under twenty-five. In other words, for every Al Gore out in front, there's a T. Boone Pickens, a Pat Robertson, or an Arnold Schwarzenegger speaking on behalf of green.

Green leaders aren't just famous people pushing a personal agenda. Many are regular folks making their voices heard. When Greensburg, Kansas, was wiped out by a tornado in 2007, 800 townspeople and 60 businesses pledged to return and rebuild Greensburg "greener than ever." Michelle Moore of the US Green Building Council, who tracked the town's rebuilding efforts, said, "Pound for pound, Greensburg is the greenest city in America." Invited by President Barack Obama to attend a joint session of Congress, Greensburg Mayor Bob Dixson said, "Never in my life have I been prouder to be an American. . . . We're blessed with an opportunity here—to be pioneers again."[1]

To date, over nine hundred mayors have signed the US Conference of Mayors Climate Protection Agreement, representing over seventy million Americans from all fifty states.[2] In a democracy, our elected officials respond to the demands of their constituents. Such a wide-ranging response as this indicates that we can't regard green-minded people as the fringe any longer.

The last time we saw this kind of public agitation from disparate groups mobilizing around a common goal was during the civil rights era. Like the civil rights movement, the green movement took decades to gain steam, but it is close to reaching a critical mass. But you might be thinking, *The civil rights movement was about equality among people. How dare you put the green revolution on a par with it?* Well, poor ecology means more poor people. In ecological terms, our actions have their own sort

> *Conservation means development as much as it does protection. I recognize the right and duty of this generation to develop and use the natural resources of our land; but I do not recognize the right to waste them, or to rob, by wasteful use, the generations that come after us.*
>
> President Theodore Roosevelt, in "The New Nationalism" speech

of ripple effect around the globe. Already, tens of millions of people do not have access to clean drinking water, and almost a billion people in the world suffer from hunger and malnutrition. Hindering people's basic rights to clean air and water can be considered unjust and inhumane.

This is an issue on which outspoken leaders from different faiths agree. In his message for the Celebration of the World Day of Peace on January 1, 1990, Pope John Paul II drew a parallel between environmental responsibility and a respect for human rights when he said:

> The most profound and serious indication of the moral implications underlying the ecological problem is the lack of respect for life evident in many of the patterns of environmental pollution. Often, the interests of production prevail over concern for the dignity of workers, while economic interests take priority over the goods of individuals and even entire peoples. In these cases, pollution or environmental destruction is the result of an unnatural and reductionist vision which at times leads to a genuine contempt for man.[3]

Rabbi David Seidenberg, a Jewish teacher on sustainability, offers this perspective:

> If predictions hold and the rising sea creates millions of refugees from coastal areas (God help us), then shelter, which should be a right, will become an impossibility. Any government trying to protect the most basic human needs and rights would find itself in extreme crisis under such circumstances, and many governments will be tempted to discard human rights in the name of national emergency. It is this kind of scenario, this kind of vanishing point in the distance, that makes me think: How can anyone ever talk about human rights without talking about the earth?[4]

Observations such as these are becoming more commonplace among progressive clergy and faith-based activists. Jim Ball's Evangelical Environmental Network, for example, represents a new generation of Christians who embrace environmental stewardship and social justice as moral obligations. The growth of the "creation care" movement started in part by Richard Cizik, the former vice president for governmental affairs for the National Association of Evangelicals, is reflected in a proliferation of environmental initiatives based on a moral paradigm to protect the poor, who are most affected when calamities befall the natural world. The United States Conference on Catholic Bishops has even established an Environmental Justice Program, which "calls Catholics to a deeper respect for God's creation and engages parishes in activities that deal with environmental problems, particularly as they affect the poor."[5]

Given today's pace of technological communications, we might expect sweeping societal changes to unfold more rapidly than during the civil rights era. No matter what your opinion about the cause and effect and the gains or losses of the green revolution—or the civil rights movement, for that matter—the world will change in ways we can't imagine. It is better to be prepared than to be left behind.

The situation our world is facing is comprised of a complex web of conditions that are blurring the lines across disciplines: science, ecology, politics, sociology, economics, and business. Having already covered human rights, we'll look at seven other major areas of concern: energy insecurity, globalization, population growth, habitat destruction, water scarcity, health hazards, and climate change. Each of these conditions merits its own book, but for purposes of providing a brief green primer, I'll boil them down to a few pages apiece. Prepare for some doom and gloom. Sometimes reality bites. But I promise there is light at the end of the tunnel, and it's not a freight train coming your way.

Energy Insecurity

We first heard about "energy independence" in America during the Nixon administration in 1970. Twelve years later we elected Ronald Reagan, who promptly removed the solar panels from the White House. Back then energy was cheap and plentiful, and global warming was not part of common parlance like it is today. Still, it is inconceivable that four decades since we recognized the problem, we are no better off. The only feasible explanation lies in President George W. Bush's famous declaration: "America is addicted to oil."

Jim Woolsey, an influential advocate for energy independence, is the former director of the CIA and holds degrees from Stanford University, Oxford University, and Yale Law School. In 2005 I attended a talk he gave in Dallas. Here is what he said: "Improving America's oil security is the most significant near-term energy challenge that the US faces. The United States relies on petroleum for 97 percent of its transportation needs. As the low-cost and dominant petroleum producer for the foreseeable future, the Greater Middle East will remain in the driver's seat as long as vehicular transportation is dominated by oil." Woolsey went on to explain that our petroleum infrastructure is highly vulnerable to terrorist attacks. "Wealth transfers from oil continue to be used to fund terrorism," he warned.[6]

In an effort to improve their reputations, major car and oil companies spend hundreds of thousands of dollars apiece on advertisements owning up to these facts. As one very visible Chevron ad reads, "The world consumes two barrels of oil for every barrel discovered. So, is this something you should be worried about?" Yes, and not only for reasons of national security.

> *Our energy gluttony is strengthening the worst forces in the world and our entitlement gluttony is going to weaken our capacity to deal with those forces.*
>
> Tom Friedman, Pulitzer Prize–winning author

Economic security is another reason we need to diversify and conserve our energy resources. Because 97 percent of our transportation sector is dependent on petroleum, the cost of everything goes up when the cost of petroleum rises. When the cost of oil spiked during the summer of 2008, the cost of home building increased by 20 percent. Utilities across the United States raised power prices up to 29 percent. Heightened food prices put a pinch on low- and middle-income families. Restaurant chains saw profits plunge as food costs increased and consumers sought cheaper options. Every time the price of fuel spikes, we scramble and act surprised, but if we look at the system as a whole, we can see our heavy reliance on petroleum makes our economy susceptible to price fluctuations.

In the summer of 2008, I worked on a project for the state of Minnesota that involved contacting companies to sponsor a special advertising section in a leading national business magazine. I saved the response I received from a CEO, because I thought it was such a good example of the direct hits that businesses take when we experience 'an oil shortage. I share it here with his permission:

```
Anna,

While we would like to participate, fuel prices
at $5.00 per gallon for diesel make an expendi-
ture of this magnitude a luxury we can't afford
right now. As a once healthy company brought to
its knees by the lack of government leadership
on energy policy, let me pass on the following,
for what it is worth. Leadership is needed at
the state and federal level that is comprehen-
sive, not partial, and should include ALL of
the following:

  1. Energy conservation: Why no action on
     changing the national and state speed lim-
     its? Seventy mph is ridiculous, yet nothing
     is being done.

  2. New sources: While ethanol wins votes in
     an agricultural state, the impacts on the
```

economy, specifically food costs, make this
option not all that attractive. Meanwhile, nuclear options that other countries embrace go unused because of a small,
powerful special-interest lobby. Hydrogen
is slow to be adopted as well.

3. Increase of oil supply: That means drilling
   in Alaska and offshore and opening up more
   federal land to drilling. Again, the will
   of the majority of the population is being
   ignored because of environmental special
   interests. In the short term, the US economy will be crippled if we ignore the reality that this nation will run on oil for
   the foreseeable future because little has
   been done to develop new sources.

Any leadership agenda that doesn't address all
three of these platforms is going to lead the
US economy to be crippled. With estimates of 10
percent of the trucks in North America being
put out of business in 2008 because of high energy costs, America's airlines being crippled,
and the inflation yet to be seen when pricing
ultimately has to be raised to deal with the
strain of high energy costs, you would think
that our government would move on a comprehensive energy policy that addresses all three
of these areas, rather than the stalemate that
currently exists.

In summary, I could give you a commitment to
an ad, but by the time it runs I might not be
in business to take advantage of the benefits. I
hold my breath that at both the state and the
federal level, strong leadership will emerge

that gives my industry a chance to remain
strong. Otherwise, try delivering packages to
the great manufacturers and retailers on light
rail and see how the economy does.

The nation cries out for strong, courageous
leaders that do the right thing. I have yet to
see a comprehensive energy policy and look forward to the day when one emerges.

Scott Arves

President and CEO, Transport America

When I asked Scott if I could publish his letter, he agreed but added, "I'm surprised that you would print it, given it suggests expanded drilling and sources of energy not typically embraced by the green movement, like nuclear." He makes an excellent point. If I wanted to be typical, I wouldn't give validity to any source that countered my own position. If you are the CEO of a freight company, fuel is the lifeblood of your business. From this perspective, it makes perfect sense to continue drilling for any oil that can be found. To others, it makes no sense.

According to the Energy Information Administration (EIA), it will take about twenty years to see any economic benefits from drilling in the Arctic National Wildlife Reserve (ANWR). Even then, it would have only a slight effect on the world price of oil, lowering it by no more than $1.44 per barrel and as little as 41 cents per barrel. The United States is currently on track to get 54 percent of its oil from overseas by 2030. If ANWR were opened, imports of foreign oil would drop by no more than 6 percent and as little as 2 percent if ANWR turns out to produce at the lower end of projections.[7]

I didn't include the letter from Scott Arves to get mired in a debate about drilling but rather to make an important point about the value of leadership. The kind of leadership this CEO is pleading for is less likely to come from politicians than from individual innovators and the combined efforts of American citizens. Drilling or not, the United States will not achieve energy independence and security unless we support investment in the development of alternatives, preferably clean ones, while lowering our consumption.

Globalization

Industry is moving overseas, and so are a lot of jobs. Countries that used to be dirt-poor have a new middle class. These folks want the American Dream too. Take India, for example. As recently as 1985, over 90 percent of Indians lived on less than a dollar a day. Yet India is undergoing a remarkable transformation. According to the McKinsey Global Institute, within a generation India will become a nation of upwardly mobile, middle-class households, consuming goods ranging from high-end cars to designer clothing. India's market for all categories of products will double in annual sales by this year (2010). In two decades the country will surpass Germany as the world's fifth-largest consumer market.[8]

> *Globalization is a fact of life. But I believe we have underestimated its fragility.*
>
> Kofi Annan, former UN
> Secretary-General

Let's think about this. We Americans want to buy our goods for the very best prices possible. As consumers, we exercise our demand for cheap goods by shopping at stores that offer the best deals. In order to remain competitive, manufacturers must go overseas where labor costs next to nothing and regulations are loose to nonexistent. This shift has helped create a growing middle class in India, lifting millions out of abject poverty. On the other hand, this has caused many Americans to lose their jobs as work is being outsourced. As an example, my husband's law firm receives emails inviting them to outsource legal work to Indians for a fraction of what they pay new lawyers in America. This is happening in every industry.

This paradox is just one of many that make globalization so complex. Is globalization a force for economic growth, prosperity, and democratic freedom? Or is it a force for environmental devastation, exploitation of the developing world, and suppression of human rights? It all depends on whom you ask. There are no easy answers to this issue. Maybe awareness is the best we can hope for. Next time you see that "Made in India" or "Made in China" label on something you want to buy, take a good look at the price tag. The real cost has nothing to do with that number. When it comes to globalization, there are no bargains, only trade-offs.

We humans are all connected, and what happens on one side of the world affects everyone else. This is an invitation to stop and think every time you find yourself becoming annoyed that things are more expensive. It's just the cost of living in the world that we helped create through the decisions we make as consumers every day.

Population Growth

Our consumption is outpacing the earth's capacity to replenish itself. Just imagine: the population of the Roman Empire at its height was estimated at around 55 million people—about twice the size of Texas. In fact, the world population hovered around 250 million for around 2,000 years. By 1776, the world population had reached 1 billion. It took another 150 years for it to double; in 1945, the population was around 2.3 billion. Less than 70 years later, the population has roughly tripled. The world's population is expected to reach 7 billion by 2012 and, on its current trajectory, is expected to reach 9 billion by 2050.[9]

41

World Population

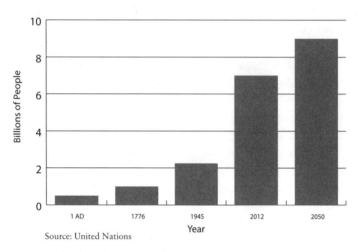

Source: United Nations

Stretched to the limit of its capacity, how many people can the planet support? Edward O. Wilson, one of the world's leading scientists, keeps this question at the forefront of his research. Among dozens of his indicators is food, which economists commonly use as a proxy of carrying capacity. Currently, the world production of grains is about two billion tons per year, which provides most of humanity's calories. This is enough to feed ten billion Indians, who eat primarily grains and very little meat. But the same amount can support only 2.5 billion Americans, who convert a large part of their grains into livestock and poultry.[10] With the developing world increasingly adding meat to their diets as they begin to mimic the American lifestyle, people in the poorest countries will have even less to eat. This scenario lends proof to the saying, "The poor are poor because the rich are rich."

Habitat Destruction

Nature doesn't happen in a vacuum. All things are inextricably linked through an intricate system of invisible levers and pulleys. It's like a staggeringly tall tower of blocks; if you pull one of the pieces out, the entire thing crumbles. Likewise, if you try to cram a new piece in, the tower can fall just the same. We can see without question that humans have been pulling myriad pieces out of the tower and cramming in new pieces with very negative ecological ramifications.

The earth has millions of hidden feedback loops, or ecological niches. When species that rely on each other as part of the food chain fail to hatch, or die too soon, other species perish. What scientists are seeing is not your typical cyclical occurrence in nature. There are now 405 identified dead ocean zones worldwide, up from 49 in the 1960s. (The Gulf of Mexico has a dead zone the size of New Jersey.) Gray reef shark numbers have declined to around 3 percent of unfished levels (the natural size the fish stock would be if there were no fishing), and they could collapse to one-thousandth of their unfished levels within 20 years.[11] In the last 100 years, the leopard population declined by 90 percent. Over half of Europe's amphibians could be gone by 2050. At the current rate of extinction, half of all living bird and mammal species will be gone within 200 or 300 years.[12]

Deforestation is also occurring at an alarming rate as we clear land to raise more cattle and to grow corn for ethanol fuel. Between May 2000 and August 2005, Brazil lost an area of forest larger than Greece. Most of the world's covered forests could disappear in the next 30 years. Without trees to

> *The constraints of the biosphere are fixed. . . . The bottleneck through which we are passing is real. It should be obvious to anyone not in a euphoric delirium that whatever humanity does or does not do, Earth's capacity to support our species is approaching the limit.*
>
> Edward O. Wilson, scientist and Pulitzer Prize–winning author

absorb carbon dioxide, the earth will keep getting warmer no matter what the other causes of warming may be.

Nearly one-third of the world's wildlife has been lost since 1970, according to a report released by the Zoological Society of London (ZSL), the World Wildlife Fund, and the Global Footprint Network. "You'd have to go back to the extinction of the dinosaurs to see a decline as rapid as this," says Jonathan Loh, ZSL scientist and editor of the report. "In terms of human times-scales we may be seeing things change relatively slowly, but a decline of 30 percent in the space of a single generation is unprecedented in human history."[13] Indeed, the scientific data in study after study demonstrate that we are losing species at a rate of 1,000 to 10,000 times the natural rate. The scientific consensus is definitive: we are approaching a mass extinction.

> *Each one of the Earth's 5 million invertebrate species plays a role in its ecosystem. It's like we're tearing the cogs out of a great machine. The machine might work after you tear out ten cogs, but what happens when you tear out a hundred?*
>
> Scott Black, ecologist and conservationist

Water Scarcity

When the water in Mali's wells ran out during the dry season, a young mother named Awa had two options. She could spend all day carrying buckets of water from a village a mile away, or she could wait in line all day to buy water from corrupt vendors. "Children used to get diseases because the water we drank wasn't clean," Awa says. "They got bilharzia and diarrhea."[14] Why must Awa and her children live in such scarcity?

And then there is me. I turn on the faucet and water flows. All day and night I have immediate access to water of all kinds:

clean water, hot water, cold water, freshwater, bottled water, springwater, and sparkling water. At my command I can have water in my glass, in my sink, in my bathtub, and on my garden. At my convenience I can visit lakes and chlorinated pools within minutes of my home. How is it that I get to live so lavishly?

No simple explanation exists for such an inequitable distribution of a resource vital to human life. Water scarcity is a systemic issue, and a misunderstood one at that. The concept of "water scarcity" does not mean there is less water, just less accessible water available to drink. The world still has the same 326 quintillion gallons, NASA estimates. But some 97 percent of it is salty. The world's remaining accessible freshwater supplies are divided among industry (20 percent), agriculture (70 percent), and domestic use (10 percent), according to the United Nations. Meanwhile, freshwater consumption worldwide has more than doubled since World War II and is set to rise another 25 percent by 2030.[15]

> *Water and air, the two essential fluids on which all life depends, have become global garbage cans.*
>
> Jacques Cousteau, French explorer, photographer, and filmmaker

Along with population growth, pollution and climate change are affecting levels of drinkable water. "Global warming isn't going to change the amount of water, but some places used to getting it won't, and others that don't, will get more," says Dan Nees, a water-trading analyst with the World Resources Institute. "Water scarcity may be one of the most underappreciated global, political, and environmental challenges of our time."[16]

Tragedies happening on the other side of the world can be abstract, but today we can see concrete effects of water scarcity in our own backyards. America's reservoirs and mighty rivers are drying up with alarming economic consequences. The once-mighty Rio Grande—the famous "Rio Bravo" of the Old West—was once a navigable waterway that swelled under bridges and made fertile an otherwise dry coastal plain. Years of drought, dams, overexploitation, a growing population, proliferation of choking river weeds, and siphoning off by farms and municipalities have taken their toll on the nation's fourth-longest river.

The Rio Grande example is but a microcosm. Similar situations are cropping up along rivers and tributaries all over the world. Lakes and rivers go dry. Farms die. Ports close. Arguments ensue. Lawsuits are filed. Millions of dollars must be spent. Taxes increase. In even worse cases, people die of thirst and wars break out. One Jordanian was quoted in the *Washington Post* as saying, "You think we have bad fights over oil. Just wait until we start fighting over water. It is predicted in the Koran."[17]

Warring over water may sound alarmist until you realize the market value of water. Dow Chemical Chairman Andrew Liveris told the World Economic Forum that water "is the oil of this century." Developed nations have taken abundant freshwater for granted. Now global population growth, pollution, and climate change are shaping a new view of water as "blue gold." Global water markets, including drinking-water distribution, management, waste treatment, and agriculture, are a nearly $500 billion market and growing fast, says a 2007 global investment report.[18]

No matter where we are on the globe, destabilization of the water supply is inevitable. Each of us will feel the ripple effects. Most of us may never understand the elaborate system that delivers water so freely to our faucets. But all of us can begin to conserve what we have so that others may enjoy their share too.

Health Hazards

Ecology operates as a loop. Each organism inside this closed loop depends on the system for life-giving nutrients. When the quality of the system declines, so does the health of those living within it. In crude terms, when we pour junk into the system and then eat and drink from it, we ingest junk into our bodies. As human beings, our survival depends on the health of this planet—and our planet is sick. In some places it's dying. The same thing now holds true for people.

Scientists Theo Colborn and John Peterson Myers, with the help of environmental journalist Dianne Dumanoski, released a groundbreaking book called *Our Stolen Future*, which provides a vivid account of how a wide range of man-made chemicals interfere with delicate hormone systems. These synthetic compounds enter our bodies through a variety of pathways, building up over years. When a woman becomes pregnant, a portion of the contaminants in her body is transferred to the fetus, disrupting hormonal signals and fetal development. Sometimes the effects are conspicuous, sometimes they are not. Some of these chemicals alter sexual development, others undermine intelligence and behavior. Others make our bodies less resistant to disease. These chemicals pose the greatest hazard in the earliest phases of life because fetal development is exquisitely sensitive to tiny variations in hormone signals. For a fetus to grow up according to its genetic blueprint, the right hormone message must arrive at the right place in the right amount at the right time.[19]

> *The danger we face is not simply death and disease. By disrupting hormones and development, these synthetic chemicals may be changing who we become. They may be altering our destinies.*
>
> Our Stolen Future

Realizing how pervasive hormone-disrupting chemicals are and how consumer products such as cosmetics are virtually unregulated by the Food and Drug Administration (FDA), we can begin to see why infertility could be on the rise. Scientists working in this field warn us of the dangers of waiting for a governmental agency, or some other group with authority, to give us definitive evidence about the hazardous potential of the products we use. "The contamination is ubiquitous," the authors of *Our Stolen Future* say. "Those who demand such definitive 'proof' will be waiting an eternity. In the real world, where humans and animals are exposed to contamination by dozens of chemicals that may be working jointly or sometimes in opposition to each other and where timing may be as important as dose, neat cause-and-effect links will remain elusive."[20]

Contamination of various degrees has utterly permeated our food chain. Thanks to Robert Kenner's documentary *Food, Inc.*, more of us are waking up to the dangers of America's industrialized food system. The Centers for Disease Control and Prevention estimates that 76 million Americans become ill, 325,000 are hospitalized, and 5,000 die each year from food-borne illnesses.

Nor can we ignore the harmful effects of air pollution. "The science is clear," says David H. Ingbar, president of the American Thoracic Society. "Ozone pollution is causing unnecessary illnesses and death in America."[21] According to the American Academy of Allergy, Asthma, and Immunology, asthma and allergies strike one in four Americans. Asthma rates in children under the age of five increased more than 160 percent between 1980 and 1994. Asthma accounts for one-fourth of all emergency room visits and approximately 5,000 deaths in the United States each year.[22]

Climate Change

Few phrases evoke more controversy than the combination of *global* and *warming*. This issue represents one of the most divisive points in America's political landscape. I didn't understand this ten years ago when I began following the discussion. I only started reading about the environment because I have a (rather inexplicable) soft spot for walruses, manatees, and sharks. I can't explain this affinity for ocean life any more than my husband Mike can explain his enthusiasm for college football. It just *is*.

Because of my predilection for wildlife, I began to form my views about global warming from a conservationist's perspective. In other words, the only thing that mattered to me was saving natural habitats. Only in the last several years have I begun to shift on this point. In fact, my perspective keeps changing the more I learn.

Reading the news, I can see the reason why global warming is such a politically charged issue. It challenges people's notions of what is fair, of what it means to be American. Taxation and regulation are several of the threats that loom should the global-warming alarmists prevail. At least, that is the perception, and in this media-driven culture, perception is reality. The truth, of course, is more complicated. And that truth still eludes us in many ways.

In case you wonder where I'm going with this, let me reiterate that I am not a scientist or a policy maker. What I think about global warming really doesn't matter in the scheme of sustainable living. And what you think about it doesn't hinder your ability to get the most out of the green advantage. I will merely present the facts and leave the conclusion up to you.

Let me begin with a brief summary. Global warming (in fact or in theory, depending on your stance) is the increase in the average temperature of the earth's near-surface air caused by excessive concentrations of greenhouse gases. Its proponents trace anthropogenic (man-made) global warming back to the greenhouse gases caused by the industrial revolution, and continuing with the burning of fossil fuels followed by deforestation.

The most widely recognized authority on global warming is the Intergovernmental Panel on Climate Change (IPCC), a scientific intergovernmental body tasked with evaluating the risk of climate change, the IPCC reported in the *Fourth*

Assessment Report: Climate Change 2007 that "global atmospheric concentrations of carbon dioxide, methane, and nitrous oxide have increased markedly as a result of human activities since 1750 and now far exceed pre-industrial values over the past 650,000 years."[23] This report was produced by 620 authors and editors from 40 countries and reviewed line by line by representatives from 113 governments. Even Exxon, Shell, BP, and Chevron recognize the report on the climate change pages on their websites.

Global-warming detractors, on the other hand, point to the earth's cyclical nature as the main driver behind the warming trend. Most deniers concede that greenhouse gases in earth's atmosphere can influence its temperature, but in a much less significant way. Some deniers also point to money—grant money for scientists and increased taxes for government—as a primary incentive behind pushing global-warming propaganda. Other deniers even call it a conspiracy being spearheaded by the United Nations.

The arguments on both sides have led to a political debate that is hotter than the heating planet itself. Since we all get our news from biased sources, it seems next to impossible to get an objective answer to the most basic of questions. For example, why does the US Environmental Protection Agency (EPA) now classify carbon dioxide (CO_2) as a dangerous pollutant when it is a natural component of the atmosphere, needed by plants to carry out photosynthesis? A simple explanation is that "dangerous" depends on the *levels* of CO_2 in the atmosphere. For example, take vitamin D, a necessary element in the human diet. In excess, vitamin D can be extremely toxic to the body.

Another point of confusion about global warming is the term itself. I prefer using *climate change* because it is more accurate. As the planet warms, some parts of the world will become colder, others hotter, others wetter, and still others much drier. For example, worldwide flooding has increased by 500 percent since 1960. At the same time, the global rate of desertification has doubled since 1970. The ten hottest years on record have occurred since 1995,[24] yet 2008 and 2009 were exceptionally cold winters. I think *New York Times* columnist Tom Friedman describes climate change best when he calls it "global weirding."

Let's say we can accept the fact that the climate is changing, and we even accept the IPCC's findings that humans are causing it. The next question is, whose mess is it to clean up? Let's look at where the emissions are coming from. Note in the chart below that the United States has been responsible for the bulk of emissions. However, China's CO_2 emissions surpassed ours for the first time in history in 2006 (although on a per capita basis, American citizens still produce four times as much carbon dioxide as the Chinese).[25] As the developing world becomes more affluent, in large part for manufacturing the goods that we import from them, they will become greater contributors to the problem. From the chart below, we can begin to visualize the real cost of buying cheap goods from developing countries. What we save in dollars on our side of the world, we gain in increased CO_2 emissions on their side of the world. In this manner, we are all to blame.

CO_2 Emissions for China and the US, 1850–2007

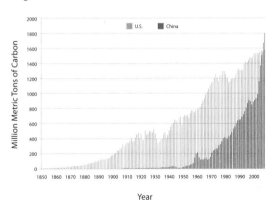

Source: www.mongabay.com

If accurate, the implications of this proliferation of CO_2 in the atmosphere are disastrous. Due to feedback loops in melting ice sheets, the melting of sea ice and glaciers is occurring much faster than the models predicted. Heat is retained by the darker surface that results when bright ice turns to dark water. As more ice melts, the added heat speeds the melting of what remains. And the more ice melts, the more sea levels rise.

According to an *Associated Press* article, few of the climate experts interviewed disagree with a projected sea-level rise of one meter. Some believe it could happen in 50 years, others say 100, and still others say 150. "Ultimately, rising seas will likely swamp the first American settlement in Jamestown, Va., as well as the Florida launch pad that sent the first American into orbit, many climate scientists are predicting. In about a century, some of the places that make America what it is may be slowly erased," the article says.[26]

University of Arizona professor Jonathan Overpeck, one of the world's leading experts on global climate change, explains, "The uncertainty with respect to what's already happened is very small. We know the earth is warming and we know that humans are causing it. . . . What we're seeing, especially in the last fifty years, is the dominance of human activity in the earth's climate system."[27] According to a groundbreaking 2007 study from the University of Arizona relying on data from the US geological survey, this "dominance" could warm the earth enough to melt the Greenland ice cap by 2150, raising the sea level by four to six meters.[28] With a sea-level rise of even 1.5 meters, coastlines, coastal towns, and swaths of metropolitan cities such as Boston and New York could be underwater.

The maps of the world will have to be redrawn.

Sir David King, UK
science advisor

Americans have been relatively protected from the impact of climate change. Many of us feel insulated due to our position on the globe. But climate change will not just harm the polar bears and walruses. In 2005, the hottest year on record, Hurricane Katrina alone caused $60 billion in insured losses.[29] Then came Hurricane Rita and, in the summer of 2008, Hurricane Ike. Extreme weather events accompanying climate change will continue to have devastating effects on property and the economy.

Extreme Weather Events and Flood Catastrophes Losses in Billions of US Dollars

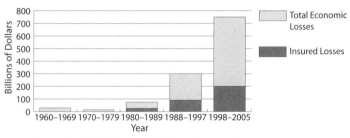

Source: Munich Re, Swiss Re, 2005, Sigma figures as of December 20, 2005

State Farm Insurance, Florida's second-largest property insurer, has already announced that it will leave the Florida property insurance market within two years because it cannot raise premiums high enough to offset the hurricane risks. How many other insurers are next?

We can argue that aberrations of nature such as rapidly melting glaciers and crumbling ice shelves are part of the earth's natural cycle, but harmful emissions have unequivocally been polluting the environment since the beginning of the industrial revolution. You don't need to be a rocket scientist to realize that the black stuff spewing out of smokestacks and car engines pollutes our air. The human body shares many of the same elements that make up air, such as oxygen and nitrogen. If pollution is harmful to our lungs, of course it is harmful to the earth's atmosphere. Since excessive carbon emissions in our atmosphere are also a form of pollution, it only makes sense to limit them.

Or does it? As this book goes to print, world leaders are convening in Copenhagen to debate where to go from here. Some argue that it makes more sense to reduce gases such as methane. Others argue that even if we do spend money trying to mitigate carbon emissions, it won't make a difference, so the real answer lies in forging new ways to tap energy with clean technologies. Still others debate the fairness of the West dictating rules to struggling nations still starving for industrialization and economic opportunity.

The big question that still remains is this: what can we do about climate change without harming our economy? The short answer is, I don't know. And if most people are honest, they would probably admit that they don't know either.

The good news here is that we don't have to wait for the big decisions to get made in order to start benefiting from the green advantage. Remember, sustainability is not a political decision but a better way to live. For my part, I'm going to keep doing what I can to live right by the planet. It may not be enough to save the world, but it does help me sleep better at night. As my friend Nancy told me at lunch one day, "You know, Anna, the way you describe it, going green sounds like nothing more than the Golden Rule." I think Nancy really nailed it.

Political Will: A Renewable Resource

Taking in the volumes of data and considering the mass extinction of so many species across land and sea, one has to wonder, "What about the *Homo sapiens* species?" Through a combination of reckless disregard, blind ignorance, intentional harm, sheer greed, or quiet neglect, we are literally destroying the ecological system on which the survival of our species hinges. Scientist Edward O. Wilson turns this hard fact into eloquent prose:

> The biosphere [is] a stupendously complex layer of living creatures whose activities are locked together in precise but

tenuous global cycles of energy and transformed organic matter. When we alter the biosphere in any direction, we move the environment away from the delicate dance of biology. When we destroy ecosystems and extinguish species, we degrade the greatest heritage this planet has to offer and thereby threaten our own existence.[30]

Wilson's grave words are nothing short of a dire warning: we harm the planet at our own peril.

At the risk of losing credibility with my conservative readers, I admit I was spellbound by former Vice President Al Gore's speech on his award-winning documentary *An Inconvenient Truth*, which he presented in Dallas in 2007. I was thrilled to meet him afterwards. I wanted to shake the hand of a former politician who had the courage to leave public service so that he could finally serve the public. No matter what you think of his politics, you might decide to admire him anyway for the fact that he saw this coming before the rest of us, and he had the nerve to tell us before we wanted to hear it. While some people still contend that Gore exaggerated, others claim that he didn't tell us the full truth because the reality is even worse. The irony is that even while Gore doesn't shy away from speaking harsh realities, he still manages to exude optimism about our ability to solve this crisis.

> *We have everything we need to begin to solve the climate crisis—save, perhaps, political will. But in America, political will is a renewable resource.*
>
> Al Gore, former vice president and Nobel Prize winner

The Land of Opportunity

If everything in nature is connected, that means we are too. Perhaps that is the best piece of news to report. Once we understand our unique role as the only beings on Earth with the ability to reason, we can begin to use reason in our approach to nature's resources. While the problems we've covered are daunting, our past achievements show that when we Americans put our minds and hearts into something, we can overcome unbelievable odds. At our best we meet our problems head-on, fueled by a unique blend of ingenuity, fortitude, innovation, optimism, resilience, and indomitable spirits. When we put these traits into action, we can accomplish amazing things.

In *An Inconvenient Truth*, Gore reminds us that we have, in fact, solved a global environmental crisis before—the hole in the ozone layer. The United States took the lead with a Republican president and a Democratic Congress, and on a bipartisan basis we managed to do the impossible. We drafted a treaty, secured worldwide agreement on it, and began to eliminate the chemicals that were causing the problem. If America was successful in solving the stratospheric ozone crisis, we can do the same with the climate crisis.

> *I was seldom able to see an opportunity until it had ceased to be one.*
>
> Mark Twain, American author and humorist

Gore closes his documentary with these words, which perfectly articulate our past successes and our present challenge:

> Ultimately, the question comes down to this: Are we, as Americans, capable of doing great things, even though they might be difficult? Are we capable of transcending our own limitations and rising to take responsibility for charting our own destiny? Well, the record indicates that we have this capacity. We fought the revolution and brought forth a new nation, based on liberty and individual dignity. We made a moral decision that slavery was wrong, and that we could not be half-free and half-slave. We recognized that women should have the right to vote. We won two wars against fascism simultaneously, in the Atlantic and the Pacific, and then we won the peace that followed. We cured fearsome diseases

like polio and smallpox, improved the quality of life, and extended our lifetimes. We took on the moral challenge of desegregation and passed civil rights laws to remedy injustice against minorities. We landed on the Moon—one of the most inspiring examples of what we can do when we put our minds to it.[31]

Those are statements we can all agree with, regardless of our political affiliation. Whether we are moved to end America's oil addiction, boost our economy, guard our health, preserve the environment, or protect our children, there is still plenty that we can do to make a difference. No matter which route we take, evidence in every discipline shows us why the green advantage is a powerful response to the problems American citizens are facing today. In chapter 3 we'll look at why the business sector sees saving the world as an opportunity, and why we should too.

3

The Rise of Eco-Capitalism

> Energy Technology is going to be the next
> industrial revolution. The country that
> owns E.T., with the most E.T. resources,
> is going to have the best national security,
> economic security, happy citizens, and com-
> petitive companies. That country has to be
> the United States.
>
> Tom Friedman,
> Pulitzer Prize–winning author

It's not every day you get to shake the hand of a living legend. T. Boone Pickens, oil tycoon, billionaire investor, and author of books such as *The Luckiest Guy in the World* and *The First Billion Is the Hardest*, has launched an ambitious plan to enroll Americans in a nationwide campaign to shift to cleaner power and get away from foreign oil. Knowing what it takes to get heard, Pickens is using his influence to persuade lawmakers and the public to rapidly shift to wind energy for power and natural gas for use in transportation.

While preparing to interview Pickens for my column on Greenbiz.com, I came across an article quoting Texas rancher Ronnie Gill, who leased seven thousand of his west Texas acres to Pickens for a proposed wind farm in the Panhandle. Touted as the biggest wind farm in America, the project has the potential to make a pile of money for both Gill and Pickens if they can get the necessary transmission lines installed. "I don't mind him making a buck, because I'll tell you what, he's generous enough to share it with the rest of us," Gill said. "And I really need it because I'm getting old and bald-headed. I really hope it'll come to pass."[1]

> In this country, we are all to blame for the predicament we're in today. . . . For 40 years, we've had no plan. We cannot go another 40 years without an energy plan. The country will not survive.
>
> T. Boone Pickens, billionaire oilman and renewable energy advocate

Laughing, I called up my friend Mike Gill and told him, "Hey, I just read about your dad in the paper!" Mike replied, "Yeah, it was really cool. When my dad joined the deal, I called up Mr. Pickens to thank him." West Texas roots run deep—Pickens's secretary returned Mike's voice mail message the next day with an invitation for Mike to have lunch with Pickens himself. "It was a neat experience getting to know him. He is an extremely interesting person," Mike said.

The "Pickens Plan," a $60 million campaign financed by Pickens, is called a "bridge to the future" to reduce foreign oil dependence by harnessing domestic energy alternatives. The thinking is that this should buy us time to develop even greater technologies. Pickens's social-media engine mobilizes a growing virtual army of voters, helping them lobby for legislation such as establishing a twenty-first-century transmission system for wind-generated power. Pickens is calling for tax credits to build transmission infrastructure as well as a ten-year extension of tax credits for energy producers. Landowners such as Ronnie Gill stand to make a quarter of a million dollars per year by installing the turbines on their property. Since Pickens is expecting delivery of 687 turbines from GE in 2011, he is searching for alternative sites if he cannot get the requisite transmission lines in place for the Panhandle project. "I don't have that big a garage to put them in, so I've got to start getting ready to use them," he says.

These are not everyday problems for most of us, but Pickens handles them with his signature aplomb and humor. Sitting across from him in his office, I got a sense of the determination it takes for one person to take on a problem that has stymied presidents for four decades. Aside from having billions of dollars and unparalleled business acumen, what does Pickens have on his side that no one else does? "It starts with having a logical argument and presenting the facts," Pickens told me. But didn't Al Gore do that too? How many politicians heard him? "Well, Al Gore's my good friend. He and I were just talking about this over lunch. Al said to me, 'Boone, we're getting to a tipping point. Let me tell you about a moment that happened during the civil rights movement. One day a lot of peaceful demonstrators got hosed down for protesting. Kids came home from school and asked their parents, "Why were those nice people getting hosed down?" The parents thought about it and said, "You know, why is that happening, anyway?" Once the kids got ahold of it, the whole thing began to change.'"

This story about a tipping point got me thinking. Maybe it took Al Gore doing what he does best to pave the way for T. Boone Pickens to do what he does best. Or maybe on a subconscious level we find Pickens's blatant self-interest more relatable than Gore's altruism. In any case, he's succeeding at mobilizing 1.6 million Americans to support his plan while inspiring his base of conservatives to support clean energy. He's also getting corporations on board. Already AT&T has agreed to convert over eight thousand vehicles, one-fifth of its fleet, to compressed natural gas (CNG) vehicles. Pickens cited new legislation as the impetus for companies to make the switch. "I know that this legislation will motivate many others, from major corporations and municipalities operating fleets on down to individuals to choose a truly American fuel at the pump," he says.

Although detractors point out how much money Pickens could make selling natural gas and wind power, they may be missing the point. Success for Pickens spells more jobs, cleaner air, and less reliance on foreign oil for America. By building new wind generation facilities and better utilizing our natural gas resources, we can replace more than one-third of our foreign oil imports in ten years and keep from sending anywhere from $100 billion to $700 billion a year (depending on the price of oil) to countries that don't like us. But it will take leadership—and not just from one person.

Wondering how close Americans are to accepting the inevitable changes that may be required of us to adapt to a world of limited resources, I asked Pickens, "Do you believe Americans are ready to adjust their lifestyles?" He responded, "Well, let's put it like this. I go into a room anywhere in the country and I ask, 'How many environmentalists we got in here?' All the hands go up. Then I ask, 'What if I said it would cost you an extra $100 per month?' Suddenly those hands go down. People are still motivated by the price at the pump, but what they don't realize is that if we factored the national security and environmental costs into the price of that gasoline, the real cost is astronomical."[2]

While complacency remains the status quo among many Americans, Pickens and his friends from both sides of the aisle in Washington are working together to find new ways to overcome the inertia that has plagued us for the last forty years. Watching Pickens sitting next to former Vice President Al Gore at a roundtable in Washington DC, I was struck by the ability of these leaders to set aside political differences to draw up solutions to America's greatest problems. "It was a great day," Pickens said in his Texas drawl. "I'm sitting next to Vice President Gore and Secretary Chu." Smiling, he added, "You know, both of them are Nobel Prize winners."

If these guys can find a way to work together, there may be hope for the rest of us.

The Richest Land in America

America's wind corridor is found in the wind-rich high plains that cover the central one-third of the United States. According to the American Wind Energy Association, wind energy strong enough to generate electricity can be found in nearly every state. North Dakota alone is theoretically capable (with enough transmission capacity) of producing enough wind-generated power to meet more than one-fourth of US electricity demand. Presently, coal, the most polluting fuel and the largest source of the greenhouse gas emissions, is used to generate more than half of all of the electricity used in America. Other sources of electricity are natural gas (16 percent), oil (3 percent), nuclear (20 percent), and hydropower (7 percent). Wind power accounts for a mere 2 percent, but with consistent policy support and an extensive transmission system, wind energy could supply about 20 percent of our nation's electricity.

For Americans to be able to enjoy the benefits of so much clean energy, a series of new high-voltage transmission lines is needed to transmit electricity from wind plants to population centers. Such a redevelopment will be expensive, but it will also benefit consumers and increase national security. Rural economies in particular will benefit from the proliferation of wind plants throughout the wind corridor.

Building out our wind capacity in the Great Plains from northern Texas to the Canadian border would produce much-needed jobs in areas where traditional manufacturing is disappearing. According to the American Wind Energy Association, wind energy currently employs about 85,000 domestic workers, both on-site at wind farms and through products and services needed to build, transport, install, and operate all those turbines.[3] The number of jobs is mounting. According to the Department of Energy, wind companies could support over 500,000 jobs by 2030.[4] More aggressive analysts estimate the total could reach 3.4 million jobs over the next decade.

Wanting to glimpse wind power's impact on a rural community, I took a trip to Abilene. Dining out with our friends the Fulenwiders, my husband Mike and I noticed that everybody in the restaurant seemed to know them.

"Wow, Blake!" I exclaimed. "Abilene is treating you well."

Blake nodded. "We love it here. The people are great and so are the schools. My business partners and I are working on new plans for expansion," he explained. Blake is the co-owner of the Blake Fulenwider Chrysler Dodge Jeep dealership located in nearby Clyde, Texas.

"So," I said, "you have a lot of business? Who are your customers?"

Blake talked about his buyers, then added, "We also get a lot of business from the wind farms. We service the fleets that haul the wind turbines. It takes ten or eleven 18-wheelers to transport and assemble each wind turbine, so there is a lot of maintenance to do on those trucks." Then he asked, "Did you see the turbines as you were driving in?"

"No, but I'd love to," I replied. My family has used wind power as our electricity source for nine years, but I had never seen a wind turbine up close.

The next morning Blake treated us to a drive to a local wind farm. We grabbed our coffee, bundled up, and piled into Blake's truck. Blake drove us past his dealership and turned onto a narrow path that cut through several plots of farmland. Cedars growing amid scrub brush, cows grazing in grass tufted with clusters of cactus, wood ducks swimming in a small pond, a hawk soaring in the sky—the picture was vintage Old West until we got out of the car. Blake pulled to the side of the road and told us to step out and look up. About twenty-five yards away, a towering white cylinder rose from the earth like a giant beanstalk. A cattle guard and a barbed-wire fence kept us from getting close to the base of the wind turbine, but when we looked up it felt as if we were standing directly underneath it.

Atop the tapering base, three aerodynamic blades gracefully rotated in unison. As the wind blew across the plain, I closed my eyes and listened to the tilted propellers softly spin. With each turn they made a formidable *whoosh*, a somewhat fainter version of an airplane taking flight as the wheels lift up and the wings take over. Loud? I suppose. Intrusive? Not at all. It was actually soothing, like ocean waves or raindrops—the kind of white noise you listen to on a CD to help you fall asleep.

Watching those magnificent white blades cut through the blue sky was like witnessing a modern marvel, one that represents everything good about twenty-first-century technology. Standing there looking up, I found myself wondering how anyone could complain about the sight or sound of these awesome structures generating clean power.

Wealth flows from energy and ideas.

William Feather,
publisher and author

"Each one of these turbines brings $6,000 to $11,000 apiece to local landowners," Blake told us. "The owner of this land has fifty. He's making at least $300,000 a year on wind power without lifting a finger." No wonder he's not complaining. Owning land in wind-fertile west Texas is like striking oil.

"The wind farms have been huge for the local economy," Blake said. I couldn't help but laugh at the irony. The Fulenwiders are our most staunchly conservative Republican friends. Blake is a successful business owner, a model citizen, and a wonderful dad—but I would not exactly call him green. So now Blake is getting on board with green power? Well, why not? Like T. Boone Pickens, Blake is smart enough to recognize that you don't have to be a "tree hugger" to admit that renewable energy has its advantages, and not just environmental ones.

The economic benefits for local economies and school districts are undeniable. The school district in neighboring Clyde, for example, went from being one of the poorest districts to becoming one of the better-performing ones in the state. As Clyde ISD's superintendent Gail Haterius explains, "Wind power has been a windfall for us because it's new money outside of the regular allotment from the state. Over the next eight years, our school district will get $10.7 million in new money due to the wind companies like Horizon." What can the school do with that money? "Capital improvements. We just passed a bond, and the extra money will enable us to build a new football stadium, a new elementary, and a new auditorium. We've needed these for fifteen to twenty years and never had the money to do it until now." Gail says the new funds are worth the change to the landscape. "Really, I like the wind turbines. To me, they're the next step up from the traditional American windmills."[5]

In neighboring Sweetwater, 20 percent of jobs are now attributable to wind energy. Mayor Greg Wortham, who grew up in Sweetwater, said that until a few years ago, everybody was on the verge of losing their land. People used to leave because of lack of jobs. "There was no thought about staying," Mayor Wortham said, "but today, you can get jobs paying $20 to $30 per hour straight out of high school. It's a cutting-edge industry. We have people returning from the military excited about what they can do here. This is a tremendous opportunity for the heartland of our country."[6]

As we said our good-byes, Blake was preparing to go to Washington to lobby for support of the auto industry, which is suffering mightily in the wake of the mortgage crisis. Blake, a lifelong fiscal conservative, was dreading having to ask the government for financial support for the auto industry. "I hate having to do this, but it must be done. What other choice do we have? America has to keep some industry here. This isn't just about cars. It's a matter of our national security and our future." Certainly Blake, the owner of a Chrysler dealership, would suffer if the American car industry failed. But so would many others: the city of Detroit, the state of Michigan, the industrial Midwest, employees and retirees, suppliers, dealers, nonprofits, the United Auto Workers, and the national economy as a whole.

I am proud to be doing my small part to support a new industry like energy technology. The wind farms are spurring the local economy, helping the schools, and giving Blake business. The ideal of sustainability may have taken us this far, but the sheer practicality of it gives us much hope for the future.

From Pumping Iron to Pumping Solar

Governor Arnold Schwarzenegger, "the Governator" as some affectionately call him, is an American icon. But he's a hero for more than starring in films such as *The Terminator* and *Kindergarten Cop* (my personal favorite). Schwarzenegger, an Austrian by birth, is the living embodiment of such American aspirations as optimism, competition, strength, achievement, and opportunity. At age twenty he became the youngest person ever to win the Mr. Universe title. Coming to America shortly thereafter, he won an unprecedented twelve more world bodybuilding titles. He earned a college degree from the University of Wisconsin and became a US citizen in 1983. Twenty years later he became California's thirty-eighth governor.

Schwarzenegger could easily rest on his laurels at this stage in his career. But if his passion for promoting solar energy is any barometer, great accomplishments are still in his future. This former action hero is certainly not afraid of a challenge. "The more difficult it gets," Schwarzenegger says, "the more joy I find in it. It's just great bringing the people together and getting it done. When you get it done, it's very satisfying."[7]

What's green for the environment is also green for the economy. . . . We must not give in to those who say that our environmental goals should take a backseat until the economy improves and comes back. . . . Quite the opposite. It's short-sighted thinking and just plain wrong.

Governor Arnold Schwarzenegger, at the Solar Power International Expo 2008

Even while juggling serious economic and political challenges, Schwarzenegger accomplished significant environmental achievements, earning him the number two spot on Greenopia's 2009 "Greenest Governor" list.[8] While in office, Schwarzenegger launched the California Green Corps, a program to place at-risk young adults ages sixteen to twenty-four into jobs in California's emerging green economy.[9] Taking a comprehensive approach to greening the state's transportation sector, he helped build the nation's most developed fueling infrastructure for hydrogen and electric vehicles while advocating for an increase in fuel-economy standards for gasoline-powered vehicles. Also noteworthy is his Million Solar Roofs Initiative, which offers $2.9 billion in tax incentives to home owners and building owners who install solar electric systems. The project is estimated to achieve one million roofs in California by the year 2018.[10]

Commenting on a 2009 report detailing the continuing success of California's solar initiative, the governor said, "The results of today's report demonstrate what I pictured for this program five years ago. My vision of powering California homes and businesses with the sun is creating green jobs, lowering energy costs for thousands of Californians and reducing greenhouse gas emissions. As the federal government turns its attention to the dangers of global warming and the economic benefits of green technology, the California Solar Initiative is proving to be a great model for the nation to follow."[11]

Solar installers and other green-collar workers aren't the only beneficiaries. Other winners include the businesses that use solar applications. Take California's Napa Valley, for example, where dozens of vineyards now use solar power. While touring us through Honig Vineyards, one of Napa's leading sustainable wineries, owner Michael Honig showed us his solar array. "In August 2006, we installed this photovoltaic system—our electricity farm, as we like to call it. It consists of 819 Sanyo 200-watt modules mounted on the ground. This system generates plenty of power for the winery, including cooling and bottling," Michael explained.

Over the next thirty years, Honig will prevent the emission of over 7,500,000 pounds of carbon dioxide—the equivalent of planting more than 34 acres of carbon dioxide–absorbing trees. How much does it cost to do this much good? "The costs we incur now are more like investments. We are applying the same money we spend on electricity to paying off the bank loan to pay for the solar panels. After ten years we will own our system, enabling us to save over $42,000 a year in electric bills," Michael said. "We used to rent our power. Now we're on our way to owning it."

The solar panels and infrastructure cost $1.2 million, but Honig had to pay for only about one-third of that. As part of Schwarzenegger's Million Solar Roofs Initiative, California's Public Utilities Commission has mandated that PG&E (Pacific Gas & Electric Company) give credits to customers who feed solar power back into the grid. These credits, combined with state and federal tax credits, make solar affordable enough for widespread use. "We'll pay this off within ten years—less if the cost of energy goes up," Michael said. "The warranty on these panels is twenty-five years, so our vineyard should enjoy 100 percent cost-free solar-powered energy for at least fifteen years."

I told Michael he was lucky. Most businesses and residences in this country don't have this kind of opportunity yet. While many states now have environmental and business leaders pressing for solar-friendly legislation, it still remains to be seen whether they can be as persuasive as "the Governator."

Green Fever

Leave it to America to turn a negative such as climate change into a money-making, world-changing opportunity. Global venture capital investment in clean tech—technology that optimizes the use of resources while reducing ecological impacts—reached $8.4 billion in 2008, up from $500 million in 2001.[12] Even amid the recession in 2009, the Cleantech Index, a market index that tracks the performance of the leading publicly traded clean-tech companies

Never before in history has innovation offered promise of so much to so many in so short a time.

Bill Gates, Microsoft chairman

around the world, soared above the S&P 500 and other stock market indexes due to surging demand for clean technology products and services.[13]

Clean technologies cross a broad range of sectors. The majority of clean-tech investment is directed toward solar and wind projects, but biofuels, transportation, agriculture, geothermal technologies, and water-related technologies are each attracting tens and hundreds of millions of dollars in spite of a depressed market. "Now, more than ever, clean technologies represent the biggest opportunities for job and wealth creation," says Nicholas Parker, the executive chairman of Cleantech Group.[14] As of 2008, the United

States was still the most attractive investment destination for renewable energy, due to tax credits and standards at federal and state levels. Germany, India, Spain, and the United Kingdom came in second, third, fourth, and fifth, respectively.[15] China and Israel have also emerged as manufacturing centers for solar and wind energy.

In boardrooms across America, CEOs and heads of investment groups are devising ways to tap the clean-tech well. I've had the privilege of sitting in on several of these meetings. One day I found myself in the office of Bruce Leadbetter, whose investment firm joined several other venture capital groups to contribute nearly $20 million to TieTek, a small Texas company making plastic composite railroad ties from recycled waste. Bruce handed me something that looked like petrified tree bark and said, "This is being used today to make railroad ties, but we've found dozens of applications for this in other industries." Made with recycled material and more durable than wood, TieTek ties eliminate both carbon emissions and landfill waste, cleaning up land and air at the same time.

"We feel that being environmentally sustainable is an integral part of our business," TieTek founder Henry Sullivan says. That's not just talk. TieTek is gaining attention and respect for taking environmental stewardship to a higher level by saving mature trees, using recycled materials, and avoiding the use of toxic preservatives. Production of 3,300 ties (approximately one mile of track) uses about 200,000 plastic bottles, 800,000 plastic bags, and 10,000 scrap vehicle tires. The production and use of the ties eliminate the need to cut down approximately 75,000 mature hardwood trees each year. "TieTek is a model of twenty-first-century corporate responsibility and innovation—recycling plastic, rubber, and other disposed products into 100 percent recyclable crossties that deliver financial and performance benefits for the railroads," says Bruce Babbitt, former US Secretary of the Interior.[16]

So how has this product been received in the marketplace? "We have more than one million ties on freight railroads and on transit systems in Chicago, New York, San Francisco, Dallas, and other cities," Bruce told me. "The greenies have been big supporters of our product."

Building Like There Is a Tomorrow

While investors and entrepreneurs are looking for the next big idea, green builders are already capitalizing on today's heightened interest in energy efficiency and cleaner indoor environments. Once a burgeoning niche in the building sector, green building is now a booming industry with the power to make and save money for America. In the United States alone, the "low-hanging fruit" in building efficiency could save the economy more than $160 billion by 2030, according to global management consulting firm McKinsey & Company. This translates into big dollars for the builders, architects, electricians, lighting installers, and construction workers who each have a role in the green building process.

When I was first bitten by the green bug, we were living in a typical brick house built by a large production builder. The house was fine, but it was hot in the summer, it was cold in the winter, and it had a run-of-the-mill floor plan and an uninspired design. Beyond recycling our trash and paying annual dues to the Sierra Club, we were a very conventional American family. But I was learning fast.

I had joined a sustainability discussion group, and during one session we discussed green buildings. Did you know that homes, schools, commercial buildings, and industrial buildings account for nearly 50 percent of all carbon emissions in the United States? I didn't. Transportation, it turns out, accounts for 29 percent.

"So you mean we can find other ways to be green besides getting rid of our SUV?" I wondered aloud to the group. "Start with low-hanging fruit and tackle the more difficult problems after that," was their response. Hmmm . . . convincing my husband to trade in his new Chevy Tahoe would be a hard sell, but a green home was something he might consider. Our family was expanding and we were thinking of moving anyway. But could we afford a green home?

One day around that time, I was getting an oil change for my car, and I picked up a magazine about concrete homes that was sitting on the table in the waiting area. I discovered Alan Hoffmann Homes, located only ten blocks from my house.

I called Alan and toured his home. "It's made with ICFs, which stands for insulated concrete forms," he explained. "ICFs are made of Styrofoam. You stack them like blocks and then fill them with concrete. The walls—what I call the building envelope—act like a giant cooler." I couldn't really tell that there was anything different about the construction type by looking at the exterior, but I liked what I saw. The design was inventive—a fusion of mission style and soft contemporary. What really drew me in was the feel of the place. It had a Santa Fe vibe. The polished concrete floors and the stucco walls, almost a foot thick, gave the house a monastic feel, but with the warmth of an adobe. To me, Alan's house was a serene sanctuary tucked away in a quiet neighborhood on a narrow, tree-lined street. An urban oasis.

> *I've been building like this for fifteen years. There has been interest all along, but nothing like what I've experienced in the past two. I think we've reached a tipping point.*
>
> Alan Hoffmann, green home builder

Today I live in a similar house, just a block away from our builder Alan Hoffmann. You might never know by looking at this warm, semitraditional family home that it is a feat of modern design. The second platinum-level LEED-certified residence in Dallas (the first is across the street), my house is eight times more energy efficient than regularly constructed ones. Certification of LEED (Leadership in Energy and Environmental Design) is awarded to buildings that meet standards defined by the US Green Building Council. This construction cost us just 4 percent more, which we save each month on bills that are 30 to 50 percent less than those of similar-size, stick-built houses.

Photo courtesy of Josh David Jordan

Our home is so solid that it can stand up against weather events that would easily destroy any other house. West Texas landowner Jack Turner, for example, tells me that his own ICF-built house has withstood the test of tornadoes that have leveled less sturdy structures. Even when weather is not a concern, the useful life of an average home without major maintenance is seventy years. Not ours. Alan's motto is "building like there is a tomorrow," because he builds for longevity. A core tenet of sustainability is durability, not disposability. As Alan told a national housing director from the Middle East who was touring one of his houses, "You know the Pyramids? This house will still be standing when those have turned to dust."

Green Business LEEDers

Businesses also benefit from green buildings, and not only by saving money. Public relations value as well as employee comfort and customer satisfaction are other great reasons to build green. In fact, the LEED designation was first designed for commercial construction and was only later adapted for residential use. After touring a number of LEED buildings, the main thing I could communicate about this national benchmarking program is that it helps builders and architects reduce emissions and waste during the building process while maximizing energy efficiency, alternative energy, and water conservation. LEED buildings are toxin-free environments with clean air, lots of light, and lower energy bills. The Jack Evans Police Headquarters in downtown Dallas, for example, saves approximately $250,000 per year in energy costs and helps save the environment by lowering emissions. Green buildings not only save taxpayers money, but they prevent smog in polluted metropolitan environments.

Pat Lobb Toyota, located in McKinney, Texas, is the first LEED-certified auto dealership in America. To earn LEED certification, green buildings are evaluated on various criteria, depending on the nature of the project. Essentially, the criteria in any LEED-certified project fall into six categories:

1. Sustainable site
2. Water efficiency

3. Energy and atmosphere
4. Materials and resources
5. Indoor environmental quality
6. Innovation and design process

Our tour guide Stefane Burress pointed out features that hit every category. For example, the exterior of the building is covered with panels made from 90 percent recycled aluminum, all of the glass is energy saving, and an enormous cistern captures rainwater for use in irrigation. Inside, the building is decorated with tiles made with recycled glass. Even the car wash uses recycled water.

The same thing is happening in the retail sector. A short drive from Pat Lobb Toyota is another landmark: the first experimental green Wal-Mart in America. Complete with solar arrays and three on-site wind turbines, the store contains many of the best resource conservation and sustainable design technologies currently available. After touring the Wal-Mart, I was handed a brochure printed on "100% De-Inked Post-Consumer Recycled Paper." The brochure details the store's green attributes, including waterless urinals, recycled food waste, LED lights in grocery cases, solar-powered infrared sinks, and about twenty other innovations that help the building save energy, improve comfort, and in many cases save money too.

Some people in the field are suspicious about Wal-Mart's green efforts, citing the harmful effects to the environment, local economies, and global society that a big-box behemoth like Wal-Mart can have. However, there are a lot of businesses doing nothing and making no apologies. Lee Scott, chairman of the executive committee of Wal-Mart's board of directors, does own up to the problem, which is the only way real change ever gets started. As the CEO, Lee delivered his famous speech "Twenty-First-Century Leadership" to Wal-Mart employees, outlining the very issues we covered in chapter 2. He went on to say:

As one of the largest companies in the world, with an expanding global presence, environmental problems are *our* problems. The supply of natural products (fish, food, water) can only be sustained if the ecosystems that provide them are sustained and protected. There are not two worlds out there, a Wal-Mart world and some other world. That's what we saw with Katrina: our associates, customers, and suppliers occupy the same towns; our children go to the same schools; and we all breathe the same air. These challenges threaten us in the broader sense, but they also represent threats to the continued success of our business.[17]

Lee's speech is a testament to the tangible relationship business has with the environment. To Wal-Mart's credit, they are already translating their talk into action. The strides they are taking with their experimental green stores, increased environmental standards for suppliers, and use of renewable energy are enough to influence green changes throughout the consumer-products sector and the related industries around the international business community. Wal-Mart has the power to have a sizable ripple effect as long as they continue to put their green experiments into practice.

A Million Trees, a Million Dreams, and Millions of Dollars

I don't hobnob with billionaires every day, but I have gotten to meet some notable ones since entering the green world. Roger Barnett is the billionaire CEO of Shaklee Corporation, a fifty-year-old direct selling company for vitamins, green cleaning agents, and other health and wellness products. He has an approachability that is unusual for someone of his stature. With a law degree from Yale and an MBA from Harvard, Roger is one of those rare people whose pedigree doesn't keep him from "keeping it real."

Roger gave a speech to a group of six hundred potential distributors, beginning by telling entertaining stories about his family. Then he said, "When you do cool things as a company, you get to hang out with really cool people. We were on *Oprah* four times last year! She uses our Get Clean products in her studios!" Oprah Winfrey is just one of the luminaries getting behind Roger's vision. Others include the president of Mexico and 2004 Nobel Laureate Wangari Maathai.

I spent five years and $20 million looking for a special kind of company, one where the daily impact of doing business can directly benefit people.

Roger Barnett, CEO of
Shaklee Corporation

The company has a total of 750,000 members in the United States, Canada, Mexico, Japan, and Malaysia, and plans to grow to 10 million distributors and penetrate markets in 50 countries within the next 10 years. Shaklee distributors are perfectly poised to capture a sizable share of the Lifestyles of Health and Sustainability (LOHAS) market, valued at $208 billion. This market includes roughly one in four adult American consumers—around 46 million people. To reach the LOHAS market, every major consumer-products company in the world has a green product line or green marketing initiative of some kind in the works. (Clorox even has a green cleaning line called Greenworks.) These products and ideas are a step in the right direction for any company, but Shaklee sets itself apart by providing an opportunity for distributors to build their own home-based business.

My neighbor Pam Hoffmann has been a Shaklee distributor for over twelve years and has built a large base of members who consistently place orders. She is now making an executive-level income from the comfort of her home and has earned bonus trips to Mexico and Hawaii. "This is not a get-rich-quick opportunity," Pam says. "But it's a proven model that can serve anyone willing to do the work."

Skeptics of the direct marketing model raise eyebrows when a company's product comes second to the "business opportunity." But the bulk of Shaklee's focus is on product innovation. The company has invested more than $250 million on research and development and conducts 83,000 tests annually for product quality. Also, Shaklee's eco-credentials are impeccable. In the 1980s Shaklee was sponsoring Arctic expeditions to look at the environmental impact of climate change before most of the business world recognized the problem. In the 1990s Shaklee's first nontoxic biodegradable cleaner, Basic-H, was named the official product of Earth Day. In 2000 Shaklee opened its award-winning environmentally friendly world headquarters and became the first company in the world to be certified as carbon neutral.

I shook Roger's hand at the end of his speech and told him I am a big fan of his company. "I use your products. I am so inspired by your company's mission." He continued to nod politely as I enthusiastically rattled on, even while the line swelled behind me with others waiting to meet him.

"You really should think about becoming a distributor of our products. You would be great," he told me.

"Maybe someday," I replied.

All is connected. . . .

No one thing can change by itself.

Paul Hawken, coauthor
of *Natural Capitalism*

For now, I'm content to use the products, although I suppose I am helping to sell Shaklee's products every time I promote them. What can I say? I want to buy from companies I respect and share the good news with my readers. It's as simple as that. Plus, Roger's words are still ringing in my ears: "We are the perfect company." Not only has Roger put his money where his mouth is, but he is also empowering thousands of others to build their own businesses too. For Shaklee's distributors, getting to make the world a better place is just a bonus.

Natural-Grown Leaders

I was standing in a boardroom at a well-known global consumer-products company, helping the executive team prepare for the launch of a green product line. The vice president was a reluctant pessimist when it comes to business and environmental responsibility. He asked me point-blank, "Do you really believe that any company does this for the greater good? Can you name even one?" Being a "glass is half full" kind of person, I talked about Shaklee and a few other companies that I believe are doing the right thing for the right reasons. But in truth, his question stumped me. Do I truly believe that, outside of a few unique cases, businesses today are going green because of love for the planet? No. But I do believe that certain people inside those companies are, and helping them "be the change" is what motivates me.

Choosing the business sector as my target audience was a natural fit for my background and skills, but I had another reason for starting out in corporate sustainability. I had hoped that working through organizations would be more efficient than working through individuals. I guess I surmised that if I could reach larger groups instead of knocking on doors, I could more quickly change more people, who have more resources and more imagination. Now I realize that many organizations can figure out what needs to be done to reduce their energy use and their ecological footprint, or launch a green product, or innovate, or be philanthropic, or do just about anything new or good. What most organizations still lack is the person with the will to lead the effort. So far, the real joy in doing this work is in witnessing the changes in people.

The people I have been privileged to work with have found courage in ways large and small to stand for an ideal, knowing full well it will not necessarily entail monetary reward. The chance to make a difference has been reward enough. Watching "regular" people learn to separate from the pack, stick their necks out, and stretch themselves past their comfort zones for the greater good is renewing my hope in humanity's ability to build the world up instead of tearing it down.

Who are these people? They are not necessarily the strongest or the most powerful. They don't always have the most impressive titles or the largest salaries. Most don't have MBAs or law degrees. They are not even what you would call natural-born leaders. They are instead what I like to call natural-*grown* leaders. They are people who recognize a hole that needs filling and act on it. They are willing to grow into their influence by leading the way themselves.

In the following chapters, you will see the positive ripple effects coming from retailers, clothing designers, computer geeks, home builders, employees, stay-at-home moms, entrepreneurs, salespeople, teachers, students, and neighbors. These natural-grown leaders show that you don't have to be a big-time CEO to make a difference. All you need is a good idea, a little bit of courage, and a pioneering spirit—just like the people who built this country in the first place.

4

God's Green Soldiers

Mankind are governed more by their feelings than by reason.

Samuel Adams,
founding father and statesman

When I first started sharing my convictions about the environment, I thought, *If I can just make people understand that saving the planet is the most critical issue of our time, we might all be okay,* not understanding how sheltered and lopsided that point of view appears to many people. Try telling a mother whose child is terminally ill that melting glaciers should matter to her. Try telling a breadwinner who fears losing his job about the plight of the polar bear. Try telling a fundamentalist Christian who sees the end times as imminent that she should care about preserving the planet.

Those who say religion has nothing to do with politics do not know what religion is.

Mahatma Gandhi,
civil rights leader

One reason why all the scientific evidence isn't translating into widespread green change is that many Americans put more stock in their beliefs than in science. America is a religious country. Whether we choose to admit it or not, our thoughts and actions are shaped by the beliefs we hold dear. Politicians don't ignore this, considering the media coverage dedicated to candidates' responses to the Religious Right.

> *I have examined all religions, as well as my narrow sphere, my straightened means, and my busy life, would allow; and the result is that the Bible is the best Book in the world. It contains more philosophy than all the libraries I have seen.*
>
> John Adams, in a letter to Thomas Jefferson

Our forefathers didn't ignore it either. They created a government that would give religious freedom to people of all faiths. It is extraordinary that a group as diverse as the founding fathers could set aside philosophical differences as they debated, drafted, and signed the Constitution. Just imagine the gridlock that might have ensued if they hadn't decided to separate church and state. After all, the fifty-five delegates who participated in the Constitutional Convention of 1787 were collectively Episcopalian/Anglican, Presbyterian, Congregationalist, Quaker, Lutheran, Catholic, Dutch Reformed/German Reformed, Huguenot, Unitarian, Methodist, and Calvinist. In fact, both John Adams and Thomas Jefferson were known to be Deists who believed in God but rejected orthodox Christian teachings such as the Trinity and Christ's miracles. Nevertheless, these men knew their Bible. The immensity of its wisdom is felt in their writings, some of which form the basis for our country's political and legal system.

The merits of the Bible are not discussed so openly today. Some of us do not relish discussing its nuances outside of Sunday school. Many of us have never read the Bible cover to cover. And yet, in today's sound-bite culture, we can find an enormous number of Christians who boil down the whole of humanity's relationship with the natural world to a single (and often unnuanced) word: dominion. On the flip side are the secular environmentalists. In the eyes of believers, these activists come off as walking billboards advertising an angry message. And when each side turns a deaf ear to the other, both sides end up preaching to the choir and wonder why they don't have more new converts.

This hit home the day I attended a business networking lunch. I exchanged cards with a woman named Sally and asked her about her work. "I've got a motivational speaking business, but my day job is in marketing with Chick Fil-A," she told me.

"Oh, I hear that's a great company," I said. Curious, I asked, "Do you happen to know how your company ranks in terms of corporate social responsibility? What are the conditions like for your chickens?"

She looked at me like I had grown horns. She gave a short guffaw and her tone cooled. "Um, let's see. How do we treat our chickens? We kill them. Animals don't have feelings or rights."

Wham! I felt like I'd been slapped. "Oh, I didn't mean to offend you," I stammered. "I know where we humans rank on the food chain, but it doesn't mean that we should treat animals inhumanely," I explained. Somehow she managed to smooth my feathers (no pun intended), and we parted ways amicably. I have enormous respect for her even though I do not relate to her point of view.

Dominion: The Power of Man, the Suffering of Animals, and the Call to Mercy

One of the bestselling non-fiction books of 2002, *Dominion* is one of the finest books ever written on the subject of animal welfare. Author Matthew Scully, an avowed conservative Republican and former speechwriter for George W. Bush, is an unexpected yet impassioned advocate for the humane treatment of animals. Scully argues that the important thing is not insisting upon equal "rights" for animals but treating them with respect and dignity. For more information, visit www.matthewscully.com.

What came up for me from that exchange is that some disagreements simply come down to the words we use. Sally balked at the idea of "animal rights" but relaxed when I downshifted to "humane treatment." Is it possible we are all fundamentally alike but speaking different languages? We may never know unless more of us learn how to translate.

Bridging the Divide

Somewhere along the way this "land where my fathers died, land of the pilgrims' pride" became fractured by petty grievances. Somewhere along the way we forgot brotherly love and began to see each other as the enemy. The resulting gridlock, labeling, and miscommunication have created a cultural chasm in America. Until we can bridge this divide, we will never get green off the ground.

> *Do we truly believe that ALL red-state residents are ignorant racist fascist knuckle-dragging NASCAR-obsessed cousin-marrying road-kill-eating tobacco-juice-dribbling gun-fondling religious fanatic rednecks; or that ALL blue-state residents are godless unpatriotic pierced-nose Volvo-driving France-loving left-wing Communist latte-sucking tofu-chomping holistic-wacko neurotic vegan weenie perverts?*
>
> Dave Barry, author and humorist

I've been trying to figure out when the most extreme voices began to drown out the moderate ones. Why all the strife and name-calling between liberals and conservatives? These questions kept gnawing at me until I finally began talking to the other side. What I hadn't counted on was for this journey to move so quickly from a quasi-objective perusal of others' beliefs to a hard and critical look at my own. The process has pulled me from the left to the center and in some cases to the right of the political spectrum. More often than not I feel like a ping-pong ball, but if that's the price of being part of the solution, I'm glad to pay it.

An Eco-Care Theology

A saying goes, "Liberals are people who know about the Bible but not what's in it, and conservatives are people who know what's in the Bible but know nothing about it." This has been confirmed for me a number of times with secular-minded friends and family, some who know biblical history as thoroughly as any other subject. At the same time, I have some Christian friends who know next to nothing about science or, for that matter, biblical history. This lack of understanding of both the theological basis for creation care and well-documented scientific evidence has led many social conservatives to resist environmental stewardship. Sadly, it has also turned many well-educated people off of Christianity.

While exploring different belief systems in search of an eco-care ethos, I decided to start by confronting my own. What I discovered among some Christians was disheartening. Some assert that God's green earth is simply too big, too indestructible to be tampered with by mere humans. My response is that among all the wonderful things that God created, we humans have managed to destroy a number of them. We have tortured, raped, aborted, and murdered other humans throughout history. We have abused, neglected, and exploited animals. And if we look at the overwhelming scientific consensus, we are doing the same thing to our planet. And in our sound-bite, divisive culture, it has become politically expedient to confuse the issues rather than bring them to light. To do so would create a moral imperative to act, which most politicians, and a great many other people, lack the courage to do.

Although most Christians won't admit this, many of us do not know our Bible. I used to be one of them, and I still am to a large extent, though it's not for lack of trying. It just happens to be a very large book. In 2005, after having my daughter Jordan, I had an unquenchable urge to test out my own beliefs. Acting on my newfound convictions, I took that year to read the Bible in full for the first time.

It's been five years now since I began studying the Bible. Since that time, I've come to understand the importance of reading things in their historical context. Written over two thousand years ago, the Bible says a lot of things that aren't easily understood in today's world. Also, it is open to interpretation from dozens of denominations. For example, the Bible tells us that God created the earth for the benefit of humankind. One oft-cited passage reads, "Then God said, 'Let us make man in our image, and let them rule over the fish of the sea and the birds of the air, over the livestock, over all the earth and over all the creatures that move along the ground'" (Gen. 1:26).

We must ask ourselves if words such as *rule* (or *dominion* from the earlier King James Version) can mean the same thing as *squander*, *exploit*, and *dominate*. In the context of the kings in the Old Testament, rulers who exercised dominion in cruel ways were used as examples of how not to behave. Based on biblical teachings, a more appropriate interpretation of *rule* is "steward." Deciphering the meaning behind these nuances requires scholarship, prayer, and wisdom.

Other passages are more clear-cut in calling humanity to care for the environment. Even if we account for varying theological leanings, it is difficult to build any case against a clear biblical mandate to protect the planet when we read, "The land is mine and you are but aliens and my tenants. Throughout the country that you hold as a possession, you must provide for the redemption of the land" (Lev. 25:23–24), or, "The earth is the LORD's, and everything in it" (Ps. 24:1).

Some passages are so vivid in their celebration of God's natural bounty that one wonders how anyone could want to degrade it. For example:

You make the springs pour water into ravines,
    so streams gush down from the mountains.
They provide water for all the animals,
    and the wild donkeys quench their thirst.
The birds nest beside the streams
    and sing among the branches of the trees.
You send rain on the mountains from your heavenly
    home,
    and you fill the earth with the fruit of your labor.
You cause grass to grow for the cattle.
    You cause plants to grow for people to use.
You allow them to produce food from the earth—
    wine to make them glad,
    olive oil as lotion for their skin,
    and bread to give them strength.

                           Psalm 104:10–15 NLT

The writer of this psalm expounds at length about the unique and beautiful habitats that God created for all sorts of life.

The Native Americans knew that the earth was a special treasure to be protected. An ancient Native American proverb says, "We do not inherit the earth from our ancestors; we borrow it from our children." As I read ancient passages, I am struck by the realization that as wonderful as modern living is, it has severed our bond with nature. Happily, people from all faith traditions are seeking to renew this bond. An eco-care ethos is as universal to humanity as is the search for God himself.

Green Believer

Before he retired, the pastor at my former church used to say, "We cannot be a club." I used to wonder what he meant, but after three years of attending this church and still feeling like an interloper, it dawned on me. "We cannot be a club" was the pastor's way of letting the people know "we have become a club." Just for grins, let's call them the Salvation Club. Like all clubs, the members share a similar set of beliefs, vote along the same lines, dress in like fashion, and hang out with people similar to themselves. In all fairness, they are just doing what people do; it's human nature to be part of the pack. But for someone who sees things differently, such clubs can be lonely.

After a few failed attempts to engage the clergy at my church in environmental stewardship, I concluded the club was not interested in something this progressive. This was deflating on a number of levels, but it opened my eyes. This congregation looked exactly like so many others: respectable-looking people in neat rows and neat clothes. I couldn't help but wonder where all the disciples had gone. In the Bible we read about exciting radicals who stuck their necks out and gave up their lives for the cause, but all I could see were people playing it safe, myself included. Not knowing how to change the situation, I gave up and decided to keep my sustainability work rooted in the secular world of business.

> *God created the world to sustain all living creatures, and in turn to sustain humanity. He designed this elegant system to function naturally, but our ark of life is changing rapidly.*
>
> J. Matthew Sleeth, author of
> *Serve God, Save the Planet*

My discouragement was extinguished when I met Dr. Matthew Sleeth. I attended his speech that evening only because I was working on a presentation for the Sierra Club (yes, another club, and all it implies). After hearing his message, I realized here was a man who could inspire environmentalists and churchgoers alike.

J. Matthew Sleeth is a former emergency room physician who left his position to teach full-time about faith and the environment. He is now a leader in the growing creation-care movement. Hearing Dr. Sleeth speak on stage four years ago,

I was bowled over by the depth of his storytelling ability. With the logical clarity of a C. S. Lewis, Matthew supported his assertions with scriptural passages as well as startling accounts of increasing numbers of patients suffering from cancer, asthma, and other chronic diseases. He tempered this with real stories about his family and his faith. In a world of talkers, Matthew is a doer—the real deal.

I've learned so much from reading Matthew's book and watching him speak, but his words are drowned out by the sheer volume of his example. Dr. Sleeth willingly left a position that offered status and material comfort beyond most people's imaginations in order to follow a higher calling. In his book *Serve God, Save the Planet*, Sleeth tells us what this transition was like for him:

> When God called me to this ministry, I was a physician—chief of staff and head of the emergency department—at one of the nicest hospitals on the coast of New England. I enjoyed my job, my colleagues, my expensive home, my fast car, and my big paycheck. I have since given up every one of those things. What I have gained in exchange is a life richer in meaning than I could have imagined. Not everyone can completely change paths, but each of us can periodically examine our lives to determine whether we need a course correction.[1]

Dr. Sleeth goes on to explain, "After I became a Christian, I went through the process of examining my life. It was filled with sin and hypocrisy."[2] To his credit, he decided to do something about it and inspired his family to change along with him. Over the course of five years, their family made significant lifestyle changes. They gave away half of their possessions. They sold their house and moved into one the exact size of their old garage. They use less than one-third of the fossil fuels and one-quarter of the electricity they once did. They went from leaving two barrels of trash by the curb each week to leaving one bag every few weeks. They no longer own a clothes dryer, garbage disposal, dishwasher, or lawn mower. Their yard is planted with native wildflowers and a large vegetable garden. Matthew calls his family "a poster child for the downwardly mobile."

Throughout the book Matthew is generous in sharing his challenges as well as his joys and triumphs in making these changes. "Owning fewer things has resulted in things no longer owning us," he says. "We have put God to the test, and we have found his Word to be true. He has poured blessings and opportunities upon us. When we stopped living a life dedicated to consumerism, our cup began to run over. We have seen miracles."[3]

One has to wonder what Matthew's wife and kids thought of this transition. I contacted Nancy Sleeth to find out. "Nancy," I asked, "did you really see miracles? What kind?" Nancy replied, "The first and most important miracle is that we all came to know Christ, not just in our heads but in our daily actions. Hanging clothes on the line, washing dishes by hand, and growing our own food are all ways of showing respect for God's creation and love for our global neighbors." That alone is a miraculous change of lifestyle for a doctor's family.

I wanted to know if there were other surprises. What about professionally? "Well, how Matthew's book got published was another miracle. The manuscript was accepted by the first publisher we sent it to—Chelsea Green, an environmental publisher that had never published a Christian book before. A couple of months later a Christian publisher that had never published environmental books bought the softcover rights. For two such very different vendors to reach out and embrace the message was astounding." This caught my attention because for so long the media has portrayed Christians and environmentalists as opposing forces. Maybe Matthew Sleeth was the bridge they were looking for.

Nancy went on. "And that was only the beginning. To address larger audiences and respond to the hundreds of speaking requests, we formed a nonprofit called Blessed Earth. In the last two years, we have spoken in churches, colleges, and the media more than 850 times." Nancy says it has been inspiring to see congregations that never had creation care on their radar screen make huge changes, and so quickly. Churches report switching to fair-trade coffee, conducting energy audits on their buildings, creating community gardens, harvesting water with rain barrels, using ceramic dishes instead of disposables, embracing green cleaning products, and completely revising building additions and renovations with a green lens.

Matthew and his wife are excited about the changes they've made and the way they've influenced other adults. But what about the younger set? "To reach teen and young adult audiences, our daughter Emma wrote a book called *It's Easy Being Green* when she was just fifteen," Nancy says. "Both Emma and our son Clark received merit scholarships to college—another miraculous way in which God provided." Raising two merit scholars is every parent's dream. (My kids are still toddlers and already I worry about keeping them on the right track.) But their daughter is not only a merit scholar, she became an author at age fifteen!

Creation Care Online

For some excellent discussion on topics where faith and sustainability intersect, here are several excellent websites and blogs:

Blessed Earth—www. blessedearth.org
The Wonder of Creation—www. wonderofcreation.org
Creation Care **Magazine**—www. creationcare.org
Floresta—www.floresta.org
Not One Sparrow—www. notonesparrow.com
Students Caring for Creation— www.renewingcreation.org
SustainLane.com—www. sustainlane.com/creation-care

Nancy has accomplished a great deal herself. She told me about her book *Go Green, Save Green: A Simple Guide to Saving Time, Money, and God's Green Earth*, which continues the story of her family's journey. "It's the first faith-based, practical book that provides simple tips for green living and green giving. I share not only ways to save resources but how to give back to those who have fewer resources than we do."

But her book is not Nancy's favorite miracle. It's the people who have most inspired her on her green journey. "We hear story after story about how focusing less on material things, and more on relationships with family, friends, and God, leads to happier, more meaningful, and richer lives," Nancy says. "With God, all things are possible—including a cleaner, healthier world to leave for future generations." I told Nancy she could go ahead and add some of my success to her list of miracles. That is the kind of positive ripple effect that one committed family can make—and it all begins with just one person.

The Green Bible

Matthew Sleeth contributed an introduction to *The Green Bible*, which was hailed a publishing first when it came out in 2008. While hosting a tour of my green home for a group of high school students, I displayed *The Green Bible* along with my growing collection of twenty or so green-related books, which includes signed copies of books by Al Gore, Tom Friedman, T. Boone Pickens, and Jeffrey Sachs. The students nodded politely as I walked them through the different topics. But when I came to *The Green Bible*, they couldn't contain their enthusiasm. "How much did it cost? Where can I get one?" they asked. I think it was the highlight of their tour.

The Green Bible, published by HarperOne, is essentially a green-letter edition (any passage relating to the earth or the natural world is in green) of the New Revised Standard Version and includes essays by spiritual and ecological leaders. Some of the contributors include Jewish ecologist Ellen Bernstein; pastor and activist Brian McLaren; evangelical scientist and ethicist Calvin B. DeWitt; bishop of Durham N. T. Wright; conservationist, farmer, and poet Wendell Berry; Pope John Paul II; and thirteenth-century Franciscan friar Saint Francis of Assisi. Among these and other contributors are experts from Columbia Theological Seminary; Duke and New York divinity schools; and Oxford, Cambridge, and McGill universities.

The most fascinating thing about the essays is the insight readers of any faith can glean from the level of scholarship the contributors demonstrate. In a world so divided by non-scholarly, anti-intellectual "certainties," the contributors—all highly educated and distinguished in their fields—are refreshingly frank about the new things they learned when they studied the Bible through a green lens. For example, James Jones, author, teacher, and bishop of Liverpool, writes:

> Up until I began to seriously study the issue, if you had asked me what Jesus had to say about the earth or what could be found in the Gospels to help formulate an environmental ethic, I would have thought, "Precious little." However, all that has changed. I have read the Gospels again and again in light of those questions, and I am still reading. I am determined to read out of the text and not into it.[4]

What kinds of insights does this biblical scholar have for us after reading "out of the text"? Here is one of them:

> The only way the earth can be relieved of its curse is through the forgiveness, healing, and restoration of Adam's successors. It is not only Christian, Muslim, and Jewish theologians who would concur with this view. Countless environmentalists, pressure groups, and lobbyists would testify to the truth that the wholeness of the earth and the future of the planet depend upon the repentance and restoration to wholeness of the human family. You don't have to believe in God to believe the biblical adage, "You reap what you sow."[5]

The Green Bible is not only a tour de force; it is also a fine example of the kind of interdisciplinary work that will be required from all kinds of leaders who are committed to "being the change" instead of just talking about it. Judging from the enthusiasm of young and old alike for *The Green Bible*, it would seem that faith is the missing ingredient environmentalism has been waiting for.

Everything Must Change

While faith-based voices are getting louder, I don't want to sugarcoat the situation. Creation-care enthusiasts are still swimming against the current among conservatives.

The movie *Jerry McGuire* comes to mind. Jerry is a sports agent, a born salesman who will say anything to get his client the highest offer. One evening in a rare fit of authenticity and self-loathing, Jerry types a twenty-five-page "mission statement" he calls "The Things We Think but Do Not Say." After everyone at Jerry's company applauds him for saying what they could not, one guy turns to another and says, "I give him about a week." Jerry ends up getting fired for having the audacity to tell it like it is.

It's a Hollywood film, so things turn out okay in the end for Jerry. Many others are not so fortunate. Throughout the ages, people have lost jobs, elections, social standing, opportunities, and even their lives for speaking unpopular truths. And we wonder why so many of our politicians are smooth-talking liars. Many people make their way by skirting the truth instead of speaking it because the cost of being honest is just too high.

> *A little sincerity is a dangerous thing, and a great deal of it is absolutely fatal.*
>
> Oscar Wilde, Irish playwright, poet, and author

Brian McLaren is one man who isn't afraid to articulate the things we think but do not say. An internationally known speaker and author of more than ten books, McLaren is an innovator on the leading edge of change in his field. I first learned about his book *Everything Must Change: Jesus, Global Crises, and a Revolution of Hope* by reading a few blogs. It took me only a few pages to discover why Brian McLaren is seen as a bit of a boat-rocker in mainstream Christian circles. "I've always had a propensity to think a few degrees askew from most people, especially about religion," he says. "And not only am I often unsatisfied with conventional answers, but even worse, I've consistently been unsatisfied with conventional questions."[6]

Some of McLaren's unconventional questions include: "Why do we need to have singular and firm opinions about the protection of the unborn, but not about how to help poor people?" and "Why are we so concerned about the legitimacy of homosexual marriage but not about the legitimacy of fossil fuels or the proliferation of weapons of mass destruction (and in particular, *our weapons* as opposed to *theirs*)?"[7] McLaren isn't being radical just for the sake of it. With an MA in English and a doctor of divinity degree, McLaren poses provocative questions from the standpoint of a thinker and a scholar who can't help but see the inconsistencies in the way so many Christians today manifest Jesus's message—the very inconsistencies that make the church appear hypocritical to nonbelievers.

To discuss these emerging issues, McLaren and other like minds have started a nondenominational virtual network called Emergent Village. Emergent Village is one indicator that the church, like other institutions in the twenty-first century, is undergoing a seismic shift. Technology and cultural diversity—not to mention Darwin, Einstein, and Freud—have made it impossible for many of us to remain in our silos. Phyllis Tickle, a biblical scholar and internationally renowned expert on religion, is not surprised. In her book *The Great Emergence* she explains how the church has experienced some sort of upheaval every five hundred years since it was first established. By her estimation, we are right on target for another one.

10 Things Your Church Can Do

1. Start small by replacing Styrofoam cups with ceramic mugs.
2. Organize a community electronics recycling day (visit www.eiae.org).
3. Share your copy of *The Green Bible* with someone at church.
4. Start a discussion group using this or another book.
5. Get involved with Blessed Earth, Dr. Sleeth's creation-care ministry (visit www.blessed-earth.org).
6. Start a "green team" to find ways to be more eco-friendly. See chapter 12 for a guide.
7. Partner with a local environmental organization like the Sierra Club (visit www.sierraclub.org).
8. Hold your Sunday school class outside. For a long-term commitment, select a spot on the church lawn and plant a garden together.
9. Involve your church's youth group in a nature hike.
10. Host an eco-film festival. Visit www.greenplanetfilms.org for a selection of environmental education DVDs.

I now attend a community church that is a short walk from my house. White Rock United Methodist Church was on a mission to reorient its congregation to the changing culture before I even joined. Today the church offers a service that mixes traditional music with a great band, giving it a more contemporary and relaxed atmosphere. Pastor George Fisk has begun to embrace uncomfortable topics as an opportunity. "A lot of people think that being Methodist means you don't really believe in anything," he says. "I am very secure in my beliefs. Most importantly, I believe that you don't have to believe exactly as I believe in order to come here." His sermon series, with titles such as "Seeing the Gray" and "Questions Thoughtful Atheists Raise," which he displays on the church marquee, are a welcome sign to visitors and members alike because they are so relevant.

While walking home one Sunday, I met some longtime members, a couple in their sixties. They told me I should come visit their Sunday school class and excitedly told me about this "great book we're reading." Of all things, it was *Everything Must Change* by Brian McLaren. After all my searching, it looks like I've finally landed in the right place.

White Rock United Methodist Church wasn't green when I first joined, but it is going in that direction. Once I learned how to find my voice, I got others on board with me. Pastor George loved *The Green Bible* I shared with him. Our Sunday school class organized a neighborhood electronics recycling fund-raiser for Earth Day. People now submit articles to the church newsletter on topics such as hydrogen cars and solar cooking ovens. It's been great to see so much interest in environmental stewardship and to know I had a small hand in making the difference.

The Way Forward

We are in the midst of the next American Revolution. You can get a little radical if you want to. Throw out the rule book. Let your conscience be your guide. What does your set of beliefs or moral compass tell you about how we should treat our planet? Are you ready to act on that?

As American citizens, we have so much power and opportunity that we don't utilize. What if we decided to recapture our patriotic spirit? Not patriotism born of hatred or fear of a foreign dictator, but one of shared love for what makes us all American. What if we could start acting like pioneers again, founding a new America for the twenty-first century? Couldn't we use our imagination, creativity, drive, determination, wealth, resources, and technological prowess—and our faith—to preserve our spacious skies and shining seas for our grandchildren? What if we act like we still believe that this country is the greatest there ever was? What if we embrace the responsibility that comes with that greatness? What if we renew our vow to be "one nation, under God, indivisible, with liberty and justice for all"?

Green is the glue that can bring us back together. Green is the path to a new prosperity, one that accounts for our natural bounty as much as our material wealth. Prepare to journey behind the green scene to see how fellow Americans of all stripes are using the green advantage to live the good life—and how you can too.

PART 2

85 Easy Ways to Save the Planet (and Money!)

5

A Starter's Guide to Greener Living

Beware of little expenses. A small leak will
sink a great ship.

Benjamin Franklin,
founding father and inventor

Widespread discussion of environmental responsibility may seem like a new thing, but conservation has been around for ages. As a child, you may have been told, "Don't forget to turn out the lights," and "Clean your plate. There are starving people in China." Some of us remember stories about the Great Depression. Centuries ago Benjamin Franklin told us, "A penny saved is a penny earned." In 1772 conventional wisdom such as "Waste not, want not" dictated the American way of life. For millennia, the Bible has preached simple living: "Keep your lives free from the love of money, and be content with what you have" (Heb. 13:5).

What changed? Affluenza took over. After World War II ended, the spirit of progress swept in, and we've been "moving on up" ever since. Just to compare, in 1950 the American Dream meant owning one car and one television. A "dishwasher" was a person. The average household consisted of almost four people. According to the National Association of Home Builders, most new homes were less than 1,200 square feet and had no air-conditioning. By 2003 the average household size had shrunk to 2.6 people. Only 5 percent of new homes built today are less than 1,200 square feet, and 37 percent have more than twice that with at least four bedrooms. And practically everyone who builds a house has central air-conditioning and a dishwashing appliance. Americans now own twice as many cars per person, plus multiple TVs, computers, and cell phones.[1]

affluenza, *n. 1. The bloated, sluggish, and unfulfilled feeling that results from efforts to keep up with the Joneses. 2. An epidemic of stress, overwork, waste, and indebtedness caused by the pursuit of the American Dream. 3. An unsustainable addiction to economic growth.*

Having already covered the consequences of all this progress, we're ready to find a cure for the resulting affliction we call affluenza. When I started this journey, I was fairly steeped in it myself. To be honest, environmental conviction probably did less to change my habits than sheer necessity. If saving the planet doesn't motivate you toward thrift, having two kids and starting your own business will. Going through this process made me realize that what I've really been doing is *unlearning* rampant consumerism.

You don't have to be Suze Orman to see that overspending is unscrupulous. But overspending as pollution, a force of environmental degradation, a menace to society? Come on, now. Surely it wasn't that bad. I thought I was doing my part by writing letters to my elected officials and recycling our trash. I had even shed genuine tears over drowning walruses in the melting Arctic. But then I would climb into my gas guzzler and go on my merry way without even realizing I was a hypocrite. Waking up to this cold truth one day, I felt paralyzed. I wanted to start living my convictions, but how? Wasn't greener living going to burn up time and money I didn't have?

Au contraire!

I got into sustainability out of a sense of duty to leave this world intact for the next generation. What sustainability gives back is a better life. As with pruning a tree, when you cut off the dead branches and shake off the old leaves, you end up with a fuller, healthier plant. Exercising the green advantage helps you pare life down to the essentials, cutting out the noise and waste so you're left with some room (and cleaner air) to breathe. Environmental stewardship also makes you a better manager of your money and time, which directly translates into more abundance. Going green is not just the right thing to do; it's an investment in your future.

How It Works

No, we are not going to start with buying a hybrid. There will be time and money for that later if you want to take it to that level. For now, I'll tell you what I tell my business clients: we are going to start by cutting your expenses. Think of it as pruning your tree. We are going to trim down those seemingly inconsequential practices that waste energy, resources, and ultimately money.

To see where the energy in the United States goes, take a look at the following pie chart.

US Greenhouse Gas Emissions by Sector

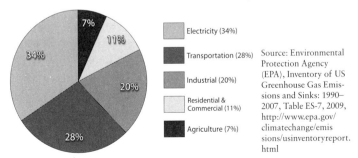

Electricity (34%)

Transportation (28%)

Industrial (20%)

Residential & Commercial (11%)

Agriculture (7%)

Source: Environmental Protection Agency (EPA), Inventory of US Greenhouse Gas Emissions and Sinks: 1990–2007, Table ES-7, 2009, http://www.epa.gov/climatechange/emissions/usinventoryreport.html

We may be tempted to think that we as individuals don't have much bearing on carbon emissions (classified as a dangerous pollutant in excessive quantities by the EPA), but the chart shows that pollution is the result of our collective everyday actions. The residential sector's direct greenhouse-gas emissions come from heating and cooking. In the commercial sector, just over half of direct emissions come from on-site fossil fuel combustion. Other sources of direct commercial emissions include landfills and wastewater treatment. Looking at buildings as a whole, we can see that energy use and other waste from residential, commercial, and industrial buildings causes over 50 percent of the emissions in America—more than from transportation!

My first observation when I saw this was, "Wow, so much pollution comes from skyscrapers and big factories blowing fumes out of smokestacks. And then there are those trucks with dirty air coming out the tailpipes." Then it dawned on me: those factories produce the goods I consume, and the large trucks deliver those goods to the stores where I shop. Those tall buildings hold offices where people like my husband go to work and make money to support our family. We may be tempted to think that we as individuals don't have much bearing on carbon emissions in the United States, but this pie chart shows us that pollution is the result of our collective everyday activities.

The good news is that whenever we reduce our carbon footprint, we are going to save money. It isn't always a linear process, and the benefits are not always direct. In some cases we may need to make an initial investment in order to achieve optimal returns on energy efficiency in our buildings and products. Nevertheless, numerous earth-friendly habits can put money directly into our own pockets.

But how do we prioritize the gazillion eco-tips out there? Saving money is a great motivator, so we'll start there. While combing through mountains of eco-advice with an eye on saving money, I told myself I'd be satisfied if I proved that someone could save hundreds of dollars per year with minimal effort. Focusing on the twenty-five easiest steps first, I was amazed to discover that the average family can achieve over $3,000 in savings per year through simple behavioral changes. Using all 85 steps in this book, a family can save well over $7,000 per year. Collectively, the potential rewards in financial and environmental terms for America are extraordinary.

50 Easy Ways to Save Money and Make a Difference

Most people think a green home is one with solar panels on the roof and a water cistern in the backyard. These and other features can be good investments for long-term home owners and a demonstrable display of environmental responsibility. However, the biggest difference any of us can make lies in conserving resources such as energy and water. Seen by few but felt by many, energy-efficiency and conservation behaviors are the easiest way to give clean air back to your community while putting money in your pocket.

To get started, here are 25 of the simplest green practices that will save you money while helping you save the planet.

At Home

1. **Replace five lightbulbs with compact fluorescent lightbulbs (CFLs).** A large-scale lighting retrofit requires an investment, but anyone can replace just five bulbs. Compact fluorescent lightbulbs use about 75 percent less energy than standard incandescent bulbs and last up to ten times longer. Each bulb will save about $30 or more in electricity costs over its lifetime. Also, they produce about 75 percent less heat, so they're safer to operate and can cut energy costs associated with home cooling.[2] If every American home replaced just one lightbulb with a CFL, we would save enough energy to light more than three million homes for a year, save more than $600 million in annual energy costs, and

prevent greenhouse gases equivalent to the emissions of more than 800,000 cars.

2. **Set your thermostat two degrees higher for air-conditioning and two degrees lower for heating.** According to the EPA, the average home spends nearly $2,000 a year on energy bills—nearly half on heating and cooling. By making this simple change, your household can save $100 per year without even feeling the difference.

3. **Use the right-size pot on your stove burners.** Five percent of the energy used per person in the United States is for preparing and cooking food. Over a year, this exceeds twice the energy a person in Africa uses to power everything in his or her life! By not using pots that are too big on your stove burner, you could save about $36 per year for an electric range or $18 for a gas range.[3]

4. **Keep your fireplace damper closed when a fire is not burning.** An open damper can let 8 percent of the heat in your home escape. In the summer, cool air escapes, so your air-conditioning must work harder. Closing the fireplace damper can add up to $100 a year in savings.[4]

5. **Use the power-management mode on your computer.** You can save up to $75 per year merely by enabling the low-power sleep modes on your monitor and CPUs.[5]

6. **Use high-speed internet access instead of dial-up to save time and energy.** High-speed access users, on average, accomplish more than double the number of tasks online compared with dial-up users. That means it takes more than an hour to do via dial-up what you can do in thirty minutes via broadband. Based on a full day's use, you could save more than $30 per year in energy costs by increasing your internet efficiency and turning off your computer when it's not in use.[6]

7. **Unplug "vampire" devices.** The typical American home has 20 electrical appliances that bleed money. The appliances continue to suck electricity even when they're off.

"Off doesn't mean off, but standby," says Mark Pierce, a Cornell Cooperative Extension associate in Cornell's College of Human Ecology. "As a result, we're using the equivalent of seven electrical generating plants just to supply the amount of electricity needed to support the standby power of our vampire appliances when they're off." His studies estimate that "vampire" appliances cost consumers $3 billion a year, or about $200 per household.[7]

8. **Read the newspaper online.** Skip the $60–$100 per year subscription and save energy and landfill space while you're at it. "Newsprint consumption is 9.2 million tons per year, and the average amount of that which is recycled material is 32 percent, so about 6 million tons of virgin fiber is used to make US newsprint per year," says Tyson Miller, director of the Green Press Initiative. "That's more virgin fiber than book, magazine, and catalog businesses combined." (This book you're reading is actually part of the Green Press Initiative!)

9. **Reduce your dry cleaner visits by six times per year.** Do all your "dry-clean only" clothes really need it after every wear? Reduce your visits to the cleaners by four to six times per year and save around $240 annually. You'll also reduce your exposure to toxic chemicals. Perchloroethylene is the chemical used to dry-clean your clothes, and this substance is classified by the International Agency for Research on Cancer as a probable human carcinogen. In fact, the National Institute for Occupational Safety and Health studied dry-cleaning workers over a thirty-six-year period and found that 25 percent were more likely to die from cancer than the general population.[8]

In the Store

10. **Buy products with minimal or no packaging.** If just one out of ten products you bought had little or no

packaging, it would eliminate more than fifty pounds of waste per household per year. This could save you at least $30 per year, as $1 out of every $11 at the supermarket is for packaging.[9]

11. **Buy your breakfast in bulk.** The more bulk shopping you do, the more you save in money, packaging, and carbon emissions from frequent trips to the store. A majority of items are cheaper at price clubs like Costco and Sam's. If bought in bulk, breakfast alone (orange juice and cereal) for a family of four each weekday can result in a savings of $300 per year. The savings on similar grocery store items amounts to 31 percent—more than enough to easily offset the $35–$45 annual membership fee.[10]

12. **Shop on Craig's List (www.craigslist.org) or Freecycle (www.freecycle.org).** Choose your city from the list for instant access to items of all kinds for sale or barter. You can get some amazing deals, and by working directly with the seller, you can bypass sales tax and shipping costs. You also avoid the carbon emissions that go into manufacturing new goods and packaging.

13. **Six times per year, rent DVDs instead of buying them.** It costs an average of $16 to buy a DVD and only $4 to rent one. Not only could you save $72 per year, you can keep plastic out of the landfill.

On the Go

14. **Skip the Starbucks four times per month.** Brew a cup at home or work instead. Every year Americans drink more than 100 billion cups of coffee. Of these, 14.4 billion are served in disposable paper cups, enough to wrap the earth 55 times if placed end to end. Plus, those paper cups contain a plastic lining made from a petrochemical that would produce enough energy to heat 8,300 homes a year.[11]

15. **Bring your own filtered water in a reusable container every time you go to the gym or run errands.** By conservative estimates, this simple act could save you $200 a year. To drink bottled water all the time would cost you around $1,400 per year. Compare that with 49 cents per year for water from the tap, which is what New York City officials estimate residents pay for 8 glasses of water per day. Water from the tap saves waste and petroleum (used in plastic, shipping, and refrigeration). "More than 90 percent of the environmental impacts from a plastic bottle happen before the consumer opens it," says Dr. Allen Hershkowitz, a senior scientist at the Natural Resources Defense Council.[12]

16. **Carpool once a month.** According to the US Department of Transportation, Americans take about 1.1 billion trips by car per day, with 78 percent of vehicles driven by a single occupant. Save at least a tank of gas by carpooling. Consider NuRide (www.nuride.com), the nation's largest online community where members are rewarded for using alternative forms of transportation. Explaining why the old carpooling model is broken, Rick Steele, CEO and cofounder of NuRide, says, "Traditionally, carpooling has been almost like an arranged marriage: 'Meet Bill. He works down the hall from you and you will ride together forever.'" NuRide remedies this by offering a free internet-based system that helps forge connections between commuters and fosters greater flexibility, making carpooling something drivers can elect to do when it suits them without being locked into a long-term commitment.

17. **Check and replace your car's air filter regularly.** Replacing a clogged air filter can improve your car's gas mileage by as much as 10 percent, saving you as much as 17 cents per gallon. Not only will replacing a dirty air filter save gas, but it will also keep impurities from damaging the inside of your engine and the outside atmosphere.

18. **Keep your engine properly tuned.** Fixing a car that is noticeably out of tune or has failed an emissions test can improve its gas mileage by an average of 4 percent, saving you 7 cents per gallon. Fixing a serious maintenance problem, such as a faulty oxygen sensor, can improve your mileage by as much as 40 percent.

19. **Keep your tires properly inflated.** This can improve fuel economy by 3.3 percent, saving you 6 cents per gallon and helping your tires last longer.

20. **Observe the speed limit.** While each vehicle reaches its optimal fuel economy at a different speed (or range of speeds), gas mileage usually decreases rapidly at speeds above 60 mph. You can assume that each 5 mph you drive over 60 mph is like paying an additional 24 cents per gallon for gas. Observing the speed limit is also safer.[13]

At the Table

21. **Pack a "waste-free" lunch for yourself or your kids.** You can save $250 a year by using reusable containers and cutting out "convenience" foods. According to WasteFreeLunches.org, all those juice boxes and cracker packages mean an average of 67 pounds of waste generated by one child each school year, and hundreds of dollars wasted. The Center for the New American Dream (www.newdream.org) also offers tips for circumventing waste and unnecessary spending on school lunches.

22. **Bring your lunch to work.** If you brought your lunch to work every day, you could pocket $1,560. Even if you did it 25 percent of the time, you could save almost $400, as well as saving on gasoline and emissions from driving. Use the extra time at lunch to catch up on personal stuff, or better yet, leave early if you can negotiate it.[14]

23. **Forget the fast food once a month.** As noted in the bestselling book *Fast Food Nation*, "Americans now spend more money on fast food [$110 billion a year] than on higher education. . . . They spend more on fast food than on movies, books, magazines, newspapers, videos, and recorded music—combined."[15] Save around $120 per year while keeping trash out of the landfill and doing your body a big favor. Instead, get creative with food you already have in your freezer.

24. **Eat your leftovers.** The average American household wastes 14 percent of its food. Each year, Americans discard more than 96 billion pounds of good food. Putting it into perspective, if just 10 percent of this were recovered, it would be enough to feed eight million people. The yearly cost of this food-waste disposal for municipalities is estimated to be $1 billion.[16] By a very conservative estimate, a household could save $200 per year by eating its food instead of throwing it away. Reward yourself with a meal out *after* you've finished what you have at home.

25. **Grow your own produce and/or herbs.** Some things, like tomatoes, just taste better when you grow them yourself. Even an herb garden makes eating at home more special. Leftovers are much more palatable when you serve them with a sprig of parsley plucked from your garden. Growing your own produce guarantees you'll save money while enhancing your dining experience.

These 25 simple behavioral changes, which are based on realistic expectations and estimates, could save your family well over $3,000 per year. According to David Bach, finance expert and bestselling author of *Go Green, Live Rich*, changes like these translate into about $10 per day in savings. If, instead of spending this money, you invested it at an annual return of 10 percent (which some green mutual funds like

Calvert can easily offer), in 30 years you would have about $678,146![17]
Compounding these conservation steps could save and make you even more. Here is the vacation you think you can't afford. Here is an opportunity to pay off lingering debt. Here is the extra mortgage payment per year to pay off the house early. Here is the money to launch that website you've been dreaming about. Here is a way to feed the orphans in Africa, give money to charity, or tithe to your church. Here is wiggle room to give your family more freedom and flexibility.

25 Easy Ways to Conserve Resources and Money

At Home	Annual Savings
1 Replace five lightbulbs with compact fluorescent lightbulbs (CFLs).	$150
2 Set your thermostat two degrees higher for air-conditioning and two degrees lower for heating.	$100
3 Use the right-size pot on your stove burners.	$36
4 Keep your fireplace damper closed when a fire is not burning.	$100
5 Use the power-management mode on your computer.	$75
6 Use high-speed internet access instead of dial-up to save time and energy.	$30
7 Unplug "vampire" devices, which make up 5 percent of energy bill.	$200
8 Read the newspaper online.	$60
9 Rewear clothes when possible. Reduce your dry cleaner visits by four to six times per year.	$240

In the Store	Annual Savings
10 Buy products with minimal or no packaging.	$30
11 Buy your breakfast in bulk. Raisin bran and orange juice for a family of four would save you over $500 per year if purchased in bulk instead of at a regular grocery store.	$508
12 Shop on Craig's List (www.craigslist.org) or Freecycle (www.freecycle.org).	$250
13 Six times per year, rent DVDs instead of buying them.	$72

On the Go	Annual Savings
14 Skip the Starbucks four times per month.	$72
15 Bring your own filtered water in a reusable container every time you go to the gym or run errands.	$200
16 Carpool once a month.	$100
17 Check and replace your car's air filter regularly.	$163
18 Keep your engine properly tuned.	$67
19 Keep your tires properly inflated.	$50
20 Observe the speed limit.	$300

At the Table	Annual Savings
21 Pack a "waste-free" lunch for yourself or your kids.	$250
22 Bring your lunch to work.	$400
23 Forget the fast food once a month.	$120
24 Eat your leftovers.	$200
25 Grow your own produce and/or herbs.	$150
TOTAL ANNUAL SAVINGS	$3,923

When I discovered that a few simple lifestyle changes could help me conserve this much money, I wanted to know what else I could do. Plenty, it turns out. Following are 25 more ways to conserve resources (both yours and the planet's). Also, in chapter 6 you'll find 10 ways to green your grocery shopping, and in chapter 9 you'll find 25 ways to green your home. If an average family practiced most of these 85 ways to save the planet that are outlined in this book, it could save over $7,000 per year!

Some changes require an initial investment. Many will save you money immediately. All of them are easier to do than you may think.

Conserve Gasoline

26. **Drive a fuel-efficient car and save thousands.** According to finance expert David Bach, you would spend $884 less on gasoline every year if your car gets 35 mpg instead of

20 mpg. If you invested that savings at an 8 percent rate of return, in 10 years you will have saved almost $14,000. In 20 years you will have saved almost $44,000, and in 30 years you'll have amassed more than $108,000![18]

27. **Take a "staycation."** Skip one weekend trip per year, stay home and relax, and save around $150 on gasoline.

28. **Switch to an electric lawn mower.** Gas-powered mowers emit as much pollution in a single hour as your car does traveling 100 miles! Also, mowers use 800 million gallons of gas each year.[19] An electric one will cost you about $5 per year to run and will also help reduce America's dependence on foreign oil.

Use Energy- and Money-Saving Appliances

29. **Purchase an ENERGY STAR–qualified DVD player.** This will save you about 30 kilowatt-hours of energy per year over a conventional unit.

30. **Use an all-in-one office device.** Conserve office space, power, and manufacturing waste by choosing a fax machine that also serves as a printer, copier, and scanner. By using a single all-in-one device, you can save about 400 kilowatt-hours of electricity per year.

31. **Hold off on upgrading your mobile phone.** If you keep each mobile phone for three years instead of a year and a half, you'll cut the resources needed to make a new one. As rapidly as technology changes, waiting an extra year could mean you get a much better phone for less when the time comes to buy a new one.

32. **If buying a flat-screen TV, buy an LCD panel rather than a plasma screen.** You'll shave about $25 per year off your energy bill.

33. **Buy a laptop instead of a desktop computer.** Laptops require less energy to produce and use far less to run. You can save about 220 kilowatt-hours and $20 per year.

Green Your Banking

34. **Bank online.** You can save around $400 in stamps and late fees. Some banks will even pay you a dollar or donate the money on your behalf when you cancel your monthly paper statements. If all US households did online banking, collectively we'd save 18.5 million trees every year and prevent 2.2 billion tons of CO_2 and 1.7 billion pounds of solid waste.[20]
35. **Choose "no receipt" to save paper at the ATM.** Instead, use your checkbook to track deposits and withdrawals. Also, arranging direct deposit for your paycheck will allow you to skip the paper deposit slip and save gas too.

Save Water

36. **Check for and repair toilet leaks.** Toilets are notorious for their leaks, sometimes wasting as much as 100 gallons of water a day! To find out if you have a leak, put a few drops of food coloring in your toilet tank. If the bowl shows traces of food coloring ten minutes later (without flushing), you have a leak. Flapper valves need to be checked once a year. If you have a low-flow toilet, be sure to replace your flapper valve with a low-flow valve for maximum efficiency.
37. **Turn off the water while brushing your teeth or shaving.** This wastes two gallons per minute! (The same holds true when washing dishes.) Instead, wet your toothbrush, then fill a glass with the water you need for rinsing.
38. **Take shorter showers.** At five to ten gallons a minute, a ten-minute shower can use as much as 100 gallons of water. If you can't part with all of your long, hot showers, consider shortening your shower every other day.
39. **Wash only full loads in your washing machine.** Each run uses 30 to 40 gallons of water. If you have a setting

for smaller loads, be sure to use it if you must wash just
a few things.

40. **Wait until the dishwasher is full before you run a load.**
Dishwashers use about 15 gallons of water each time
you run them. Make it count by running them full.

41. **Fix dripping faucets.** A slow drip can waste 15 to 20
gallons a day. Often you need only to replace a washer
to stop a drip.

42. **Reuse water when you can.** For example, when you
rinse out the coffee pot or a glass, that water can be
used to water plants.

43. **Water your lawn, garden, and landscape early in the
morning when evaporation rates are at their lowest.**
When you water in the heat of the day, you can lose 40
to 60 percent of the water to evaporation.

44. **Use a bucket of water to wash your pet.** A continuously
running hose can dispense up to 75 gallons of water in
just 15 minutes—300 gallons in an hour.

45. **Use a broom, not a hose, to clean driveways and side-
walks.** You'll save water and get some exercise too!

46. **Water only when the lawn begins to show signs of stress.**
Look for discoloration, wilting, or footprints that remain
visible after someone has walked across the lawn. Most
people grossly overwater. Infrequent watering will help
your lawn develop a deep and healthy root system.

47. **Xeriscape your lawn.** Plant native or adapted plants that
don't require extra water. Reduce grassy areas with rocks
and other natural materials to add visually appealing
texture to your terrain. You'll save water, money, time,
and energy from not having to mow as much yard.

Reduce, Reuse, and Recycle

48. **Practice the 3 R's.** For every action, consider how you
can reduce, reuse, and recycle. Reuse gift wrap. Rinse
out Ziploc bags. You will save pennies and dollars every
time, as well as untold amounts of waste. Just consider

a single aluminum can. It takes seven times more energy to produce one made from virgin ore as it does to make one from recycled material. The United States still gets three-fifths of its aluminum from virgin ore, at twenty times the intensity of recycled aluminum, and we throw away enough aluminum to replace our entire commercial aircraft fleet every three months![21]

49. **Buy recycled products.** Products that use recycled paper preserve virgin forests, which are vital to staving off climate change and habitat loss. Recycled paper products can even save you money. For example, Seventh Generation's recycled-fiber toilet paper costs less per square foot than most leading brands.

50. **Mix your own products.** Mixing your own biodegradable potions with all-natural products from your pantry can save you over $500 per year. Using common ingredients, you can mix your own cleaning agents and personal-care products. Altuse (www.altuse.com) can help you tap into the planet's collective wisdom so you can keep more in your wallet and send less to landfills. It offers recipes and tips for using hairspray to remove ink stains, vodka to clean your eyeglasses, coffee grounds to fertilize your garden, and hundreds of other applications for everyday household substances and items.

The New American Dream

The Center for the New American Dream explains its mission like this: "We envision a society that values not just 'more' but more of what matters."[22] This group sponsors wonderful campaigns to connect thousands of innovators, activists, busy parents, college students, and avid professionals striving to live consciously, buy wisely, and make a difference. Similar groups across the country are springing up with the goal of helping Americans overcome consumerism and embrace simplicity. I'm thrilled to see this kind of support available. I wish I had known about it six years ago.

When my own family went through the simplification process, I felt like an oddball. We were a two-income family with two car payments and seven credit cards. We had great vacations, designer clothes, and a good time. Only in hindsight can I see how the endless game of "keeping up" kept me too busy to see that we were going nowhere. Wanting to inject purpose back into my life, I left my career as an IBM consultant. Admittedly, the journey from full-time employment to self-employment wasn't easy. We didn't go on vacation for five years. Determined to get out of debt, we halted 90 percent of our recreational spending for four years. The designer labels from Neiman Marcus dwindled into "designer wear" from Target. My once-new car morphed from merely used to nearly vintage.

> As you simplify your life, the laws of the universe will be simpler; solitude will not be solitude, poverty will not be poverty, nor weakness weakness.
>
> Henry David Thoreau, American author, philosopher, and naturalist

What had started out as difficult ended up being a blessing. Looking back, I see how all the spending caused a lot of anxiety. Today I've found that I am satisfied with less stuff, not to mention less stress. Luxury has taken on a whole new meaning. We have two beautiful children. We own both cars and can get by on my husband's income, with mine providing the extras. We've cut up our credit cards, and we're working toward becoming debt free. We built a green home where we love to spend our time. My children's school and our church are within walking distance. I work from home while doing what I love. By a strict environmentalist's standards, we're still taking baby steps. But by ours, this is a big leap forward. We're still living the good life, just doing it in a greener way.

I laugh when I remember my first reaction to Thoreau's life on Walden, where the American writer went to retreat from all the materialism and live off the land for two years. I couldn't imagine something so dull, with nothing to do but write and contemplate the birds and trees. Today I devote a lot of time to contemplation, and I enjoy nature more fully than ever. We're not exactly living off the land, but I do have a vegetable garden. Exercising the green advantage has helped us reduce our environmental burden as well as our stress load. What else can I say? In a nutshell: spend less, savor more—it's the new American Dream.

6

Organic Cuisine, Sustainable Wine, and Local Flavor

> Tell me what you eat, and I shall tell you what you are.
>
> Jean-Anthelme Brillat-Savarin,
> author of *The Physiology of Taste*

If you are trying to live the good life in a greener way, begin by investing in better eating habits. You'll experience immediate returns in improved health and better taste. I can vouch from experience. When I first entered the green scene, we were conventional shoppers. I used to buy all the "normal" commercial brands at the grocery store. I generally avoided the health food aisle and sneered at terms like "vegan" and "gluten free." (I didn't know what gluten was, but I was pretty sure it belonged in my potato chips.) And I had no qualms about toting home my conventionally grown bananas in plastic grocery bags. But after discovering the pleasure of delicacies like locally grown, vine-ripened tomatoes fresh from the farmer's market, I'm now a true believer in quality over convenience.

If I can change, there's hope for the rest of us. And based on the evidence, a lot of us could benefit from making some changes. Consider the statistics:

- Americans spend over half of every food dollar on ready-prepared, ready-to-eat food, most of which is high in added fats and sugars.
- On any given day, one-quarter of US adults eat fast food.
- US consumption of high-fructose corn syrup (an added sugar) increased over 1,000 percent in the last 30 years.
- US consumption of added fats shot up more than 35 percent in that same period.
- The average American consumes over 50 gallons of carbonated soft drinks a year.
- Nearly one-third of our calories comes from junk food.
- A full one-third of US vegetable consumption consists of frozen potatoes (mostly French fries), potato chips, and iceberg lettuce.[1]

Our convenience-based approach to cuisine is unhealthy, unsavory, and ultimately unsatisfying.

On the other hand, we have the French. Much ado has been made about the "French paradox," or Mediterranean diet. Although eating a baguette slathered with real butter while swilling wine seems counterintuitive to diet-conscious Americans, if we step back and look at this logically, it begins to make sense. The French motto is "everything in moderation." They eat what they like, but they do so in smaller portions. They don't go back for seconds. They don't snack. They seldom eat alone. Communal meals are long, leisurely affairs. They eat fewer prepared frozen foods. They are more apt to buy local. Learning from these habits brings us closer to greener eating, not to mention genuine feasting.

When our sustainability discussion group first started reading the guide from Northwest Earth Institute called "Choices for Sustainable Living," I quickly realized that in spite of my good intentions, my diet was far from green. As a shopper, I regularly committed green shopping infractions without even knowing it. Rather than shaming me, group members laughed and made their own confessions. We were there not to judge but to support each other and learn what to look for, what to buy, where to shop, and what the health benefits were. The more I learned, the easier it became to make the shift. Knowledge is power, and a knowledgeable consumer is a more powerful citizen.

Buying green is like voting with your dollars. It's also an excellent way to give your family the healthy, rich, and flavorful dining experience they deserve.

Northwest Earth Institute

The Northwest Earth Institute (NWEI) is a national leader in the development of innovative programs empowering individuals and organizations to protect ecological systems. NWEI offers eight study guides for small groups. These self-guided discussion courses are offered in workplaces, universities, homes, faith centers, neighborhoods, and community centers throughout North America. Each program encourages participants to explore values, attitudes, and actions through discussion with other people.

For more information, visit www.nwei.org.

Why Greener Eating?

As an advocate for sustainability, my initial decision to incorporate organic foods into my diet had more to do with helping the planet than with safeguarding my health. Like most Americans, I assumed that the food and beverages stocked on the grocery store shelves must be okay. I mean, the brands are advertised everywhere and pass government inspection, right?

Or was I putting a little too much stock in a system that was not capable of looking out for my long-term interests?

Only during my pregnancy did I begin to look more closely at my diet. Becoming a parent convinced me to take an active role in educating myself about healthy eating. As I learned about the food chain, the abstract, science-based reasoning covered in chapter 2 suddenly took on an urgent and practical significance. All at once, I could see how environmental degradation was directly harming us humans. The evidence was sitting on my plate.

Take eggs, for example. A study completed in 2007 by the Mother Earth News egg-testing project found that, when compared with conventional eggs, eggs from hens raised on pasture contain one-third less cholesterol, one-fourth less saturated fat, two-thirds more vitamin A, two times more omega fatty acids, three times more vitamin E, and seven times more beta carotene! The natural diet of seeds, green plants, insects, worms, and grain directly contributes to more nutrient-rich eggs than the cheap mixture of corn, soy, and/ or cottonseed meals with additives.[2] It just goes to show that Mother Nature knows best, and we get the best when we rely on her as much as possible for our food.

Of course, responsible eating isn't always cut-and-dried or convenient. Zoe Bradbury, a Food and Society policy fellow who lives in Oregon, explains how nerve-racking a quick trip to buy eggs can become when you set out to do the right thing. "Does one semitruck delivering whole pallets of eggs from California have a smaller carbon footprint than ten local farmers driving to town twice a week to deliver a couple crates of eggs in their own pickups?" Bradbury wonders. "And what kind of conditions do the chickens live in? Is it humane? What are they fed? Can I believe the label? What's the most nutritious egg for my body? Is the healthiest one the most expensive one?"[3] Thinking it through to this extreme makes shopping as difficult as studying for the SATs.

What Is So Wrong with Fertilizer?

Synthetic fertilizers such as Miracle Gro are by-products of the petroleum industry and are almost always overkill. Runoff of fertilizer chemicals pollutes streams and water supplies. Using too much synthetic fertilizer can burn plants, hurt the soil, and damage your earthworm population.

Conversely, organic fertilizers such as fish emulsion, bone meal, and kelp meal will feed organisms that live in soil and plant roots. Worm castings, manure, compost, and organic fertilizers are full of beneficial microbes, good bacteria, and fungi. Adding these organic products to the soil means you feed the soil, not just the plant.

Synthetic fertilizers are a pill; they contain only a few major nutrients. To your soil, organic fertilizers are a complete meal.

When it comes to buying groceries, I don't have quite the moral quandary that Zoe does. I've made a decision not to overthink it. Instead of using a rigid set of rules, I operate according to a set of flexible principles when buying food. Faced with conventional choices and a fixed budget, we sometimes have to settle for "less bad" when we can't have the best. Also, as with alternative energy, there is no single solution to environmentally responsible eating. Even the good ideas can have not-so-good trade-offs (such as the organic apple flown in from two thousand miles away versus the locally but conventionally grown one from the farmer's market). Instead of attempting a strictly organic diet, I strive for greener eating. Truly green is hard to pull off, but we can all be greener.

Greener Grocery Shopping

Following are 10 principles to greener grocery shopping that will help you make the easiest, healthiest decisions possible without spending all day (and all your money) at the store.

1. **Plan meals before you go grocery shopping.** You will be less likely to reach for frozen, processed, and prepackaged

foods if you already know which recipes you will use to cook your meals. Take inventory of the ingredients in your pantry and keep a list handy of those you still need to buy.

2. **Prepare more meals without meat.** If you love meat, you don't have to give it up, but easing up on meat consumption is good for your health and conserves resources for others too. If Americans reduced their meat consumption by just 10 percent, enough grain would be saved to feed 60 million people. This is close to the total number of those who die of hunger-related disease each year! Again, with a little advance planning, you can prepare delectable, protein-rich vegetarian meals without even missing the meat.[4]

3. **Shop the perimeter of the store first.** Fill your cart first with fresh food like produce, eggs, cheese, meat, and milk. This will leave less room for processed, overpackaged, and costly foods from the aisles.

4. **Look for labels with third-party verification.** Labels such as "natural," "cage free," and "free range" don't tell us everything we want to know because they lack specific standards. For example, "free range" implies that a bird was free to roam when, in reality, it may have had very limited access to the outdoors. The best labels will have a third-party verification associated with them, demonstrating greater accountability and accuracy. Learning your labels will help you become an informed shopper. It will also help you get higher quality and more value for your shopping dollars.

5. **Buy organic versions of fruits and vegetables most often contaminated by pesticides.** According to the Environmental Working Group, the following are most affected by pesticides: peaches, apples, cherries, lettuce, bell peppers, grapes, celery, pears, nectarines, spinach, strawberries, and potatoes. Buying organic produce also helps keep you from contributing to water pollution

through agricultural runoff. Remember the dead zones in the oceans from chapter 2? It has been estimated that as much as 25 percent of fertilizer spread on farmland each year is lost as runoff. When the nitrogen in fertilizer is not used in growing plants, runoff containing nitrates drastically affects water health. For example, each spring and summer a 7,000-square-mile dead zone develops in the northern Gulf of Mexico due to excess nitrogen, stripping the water of oxygen.[5] Buying organic is not more "expensive"; rather, it's an investment in your family's health.

6. **Buy 100-percent-certified organic dairy products.** Recombinant bovine growth hormone, shortened to rBGH (or rBST), is a genetically engineered hormone injected into dairy cows to increase their milk production. This hormone stimulates the growth of another one called IGF-1. These hormones have been linked to cysts as well as colon, breast, and smooth-muscle cancers. The United States is one of the few countries whose dairy farmers use rBGH, which is not approved for use in Canada, the European Union, New Zealand, or Australia.[6] (The FDA did not require human testing as part of the approval process.) Some labels to look for while shopping include "Horizon" and "Organic Valley" milk and cheese.

> **BlueAvocado** has developed the "gro-pak" for grocery shopping that includes everything from large multiuse bags to stylish totes to ventilated produce bags. They offer four combinations to help you haul, ventilate, and insulate your food. The entire system folds into a tight little "pak" to keep in your car or purse.
>
> For more information, visit www.blueavocado.com.

7. **Look for the "Fish Forever" seal.** An estimated 75 percent of the world's fish species are either being caught at maximum levels or are near collapse from overfishing. Populations of tuna, swordfish, cod, and halibut have been reduced by 90 percent worldwide.[7]

The "Fish Forever" seal from the Marine Stewardship Council indicates that fish come from a well-managed fishery with healthy populations that are not damaging ocean ecosystems. Alaskan salmon, for instance, are known to be sustainable since fish farms are not allowed. Also, fish like these are not in danger of being contaminated with mercury and polychlorinated biphenyls (PCBs).

8. **Buy more of your groceries in bulk.** In chapter 5, I reported that a family of four could save over $500 by simply purchasing breakfast food in bulk. Try doing this for more of your household items. By some estimates, you will reduce your annual grocery bills by a third.[8] While buying in bulk doesn't always translate into a smaller carbon footprint, you will certainly reduce the amount of packaging you waste. Also, Sam's Club and Costco carry paper towels and toilet paper with recycled content. Remember, the more you demand green products, the more likely these stores will be to stock them.

9. **Shop at your local farmer's market or community-supported agriculture (CSA).** Even though it's not always organic, locally sourced produce is likely to be fresher because it hasn't had to travel so far, which also means the carbon footprint is smaller. Because it comes straight from the farm, the produce tastes better and supports local economies. Also, it's more fun to shop outdoors while speaking to the very people who grow your food.

10. **Bring your own bags.** Don't wreck a great green shopping spree by toting home your groceries in plastic bags. Bring your own instead. Remember, it takes twenty-one days to create a new habit, so don't be surprised if you forget to bring your bags with you at first. Try to keep them somewhere visible in your car to help you remember.

The Hidden Benefits of Vegan Cuisine

Sold on organic, but still unsure about vegetarian or vegan cuisine? If you are, I can relate. Ironically, I used to be suspicious of people who didn't eat meat because it didn't seem natural. But since getting educated on the health, environmental, and economic drawbacks of Americans' meat intake, I've become

Labels Supported by Third-Party Verification

- **"American Humane Certified"** assures humane care of livestock and no use of growth hormones or nontherapeutic antibiotics. Applies to meat, poultry, eggs, and dairy.
- **"Bird Friendly"** protects tropical bird habitats. Used for coffee.
- **"Certified Humane Raised & Handled"** verifies that animals have had access to clean and sufficient food and water, a safe environment, protection from foul weather, and space to move naturally. Applies to meat, poultry, egg, and dairy products.
- **"Certified Organic"** means farms must follow strict standards set by the USDA's national organic standard, prohibiting the use of antibiotics, synthetic hormones, and pesticides. Products containing 95 percent organic ingredients may be labeled "organic," but only those with 100 percent organic ingredients can use USDA's Certified Organic seal.
- **"Fair Trade Certified"** ensures farmers receive fair prices. Applies to coffee, tea, chocolate, tropical fruit, rice, and sugar.
- **"Food Alliance Certified"** indicates sustainable farming practices, soil and water conservation, and fair treatment of workers. Applies to milk, frozen food, fruit, wheat, meat, and vegetables.
- **"Free-Farmed"** means animals had access to clean food and water and were raised without antibiotics to promote growth. Applies to meat and poultry.
- **"Grass-Fed"** guarantees livestock received continuous access to natural outdoor forage during the growing season. Applies to dairy, beef, and lamb.
- **"Marine Stewardship Council"** signifies well-managed fisheries. Applies to farmed and wild-caught fish.
- **"Rain Forest Alliance"** protects rain forests.
- **"Salmon-Safe"** protects watersheds.[9]

more curious about vegetarian cuisine. If you want to hear from someone who makes vegetarian and vegan food sound delicious and satisfying, look no further than Deirdre Imus, bestselling author and cofounder of the groundbreaking Deirdre Imus Environmental Center for Pediatric Oncology.

Deirdre and her husband Don, host of the nationally syndicated talk show *Imus in the Morning*, created the nonprofit Imus Cattle Ranch for Kids with Cancer. Interviewing Deirdre, I was struck by how she has managed to funnel her passion for health and fitness into a rare and special place that helps children cope with cancer and other environmental-related illnesses. "Ours is the only working cattle ranch in America that we know of to be organic and vegan," Deirdre said. "To some, a vegan cattle ranch may seem a contradiction, but then so would a place where desperately ill children discover their true strength by learning to ride horses and rope calves."

The ranch represents a way to help kids cope with the consequences of diseases that are the result of environmental degradation. Deirdre cited some astonishing statistics. "There is a 31 percent increase in cancer among children. One in six kids is obese. One in six kids has asthma. One in eight children is born premature. One in sixty boys is diagnosed with autism. We've seen rapid growth in Tourette's syndrome and diabetes. Another chronic disease growing among children is arthritis. These statistics are hard facts. Why is this generation of children sicker than other children?" she asked. "Many factors that contribute to this startling increase are environmental. This is the reality. So I began to focus on one area where I could make a significant impact: food. Our food chain has been destroyed. This is the root of where all my work in the green arena blossomed."

Deirdre's commitment to a vegan diet has a long history. "I've been a vegan for twenty-five years," she told me. "Back in high school as a runner, I discovered I could perform better and feel better with a vegetable and plant-based diet. So I've been living this way for several decades. That is how it was so natural to weave it into the business." She added, "Our ranch in New Mexico is completely non-toxic. We have seventeen buildings built to state-of-the-art green standards. We have around five thousand acres with a working farm of horses, chickens, donkeys, sheep, and cattle. We don't spray any pesticides. In fact, we're working on applying for biodynamic certification. We are confident that everything we serve these kids from our ranch is organic and toxin-free. In fact, every substance that we can control, from fly sprays and mosquito repellants to our Greening the Cleaning products, is nontoxic and organic."

For Deirdre, contributing to a healthy environment is more a calling than a hobby. As with her books, Deirdre uses sales of her product line to generate revenue for the ranch. "Our work extends beyond protecting the physical environment. Part of being green for me is creating a nurturing and healing environment for kids to recover. This is our eleventh year of having the kids out for the summer," she said, smiling. "We love being able to assign the kids their own horses and teach them how to feed, care for, and ride them. They love it and we love it."

The Imus Ranch: Cooking for Kids and Cowboys

In her book *The Imus Ranch*, Deirdre shares more than 125 recipes from this very special place she and her husband created together. The vegan dishes are meant to be prepared from produce as close to fresh and homegrown as what the Imuses serve from their own garden. The dishes—from Butch's Blueberry Pancakes, Cowboy Sloppy Joes, and Buffalo Red Chili Enchiladas to Chickenless Pot Pie, Imus Ranch Barbecue, and Walnut Chocolate Chip Cookies—are guaranteed to please the whole family.

Visit www.dienviro.com and www.imusranchfoods.com for more information on Deirdre's books, cleaning products, and specialty foods. One hundred percent of all profits go to the Imus Cattle Ranch for Kids with Cancer in Ribera, New Mexico.

Sustainable Wine for Dummies

"Dining provides one of life's great pleasures," says Robert Mondavi, one of America's great winemakers. "It allows people the opportunity to savor each other's company, to develop and refine the art of conversation, and get in touch with the sensory aspects of life." Those of us on the road to greening the good life may delight in knowing that wines, too, can be sustainable. More organic and sustainable wine labels are cropping up in places such as Whole Foods, although for some of us, this can make wine buying even more complicated.

My husband and I love wine, but we are by no means connoisseurs. Even after buying *Wine for Dummies*, I still find myself asking questions such as, "How do you recognize a good wine?" and "Which matters more—varietal or region?" Compounding my confusion, I now have green questions too: "How do organic grapes improve a wine?" and "What makes a vineyard sustainable?" A little education had greatly enhanced my experience with food, so I knew the same would hold true for wine.

There's no better place in America to learn about wines than California's Napa Valley. We had been to Napa eight years prior, before we had green on our radar. This time we decided to explore California's wine country while looking through the green lens.

As I write this, I'm overlooking one of Napa Valley's 340 or so wineries. (The state of California has around 2,700,

Green Beer: It's Not Just for St. Patrick's Day Anymore

Not a wine drinker? Try these eco-friendly habits to green your beer consumption:

1. Buy locally produced beer that hasn't been shipped for long distances.
2. Brew your own organic beer (visit www.breworganic.com).
3. Use kegs or growlers when hosting a party to reduce waste of glass bottles and aluminum cans.
4. Evaluate the organic beers available at a store near you. See the Beer Buying Guide at www.thegreenguide.com/buying-guide/beer.

roughly half the total number in the country.) It's a sunny day and the temperature is close to 70 degrees. Rows upon rows of grapevines roll across the valley's slopes. "For purple mountain majesties above the fruited plain . . ." Whoever wrote those lyrics to "America the Beautiful" had to be thinking about California.

After three days of visiting vineyards, I've learned wine appreciation is like peeling the layers of an onion. Just when you think you've got it down, you realize you've only brushed the surface. Wondering if I'm alone, I asked a wine server in one of the tasting rooms, "Do most people who come here genuinely recognize the nuances of wines?" She laughed and said, "Not at all. Maybe 5 percent of the visitors I meet in Napa really know their stuff (which translates to way less than 1 percent of Americans). The rest are here for enjoyment. In fact, you're always learning, and your taste will always be evolving. It's a journey." It's a relief to know that novices are made to feel welcome in Napa Valley.

Sustainable winemaking isn't new to Napa, but what was once considered a trend seems poised to become an industry standard. To clarify, *sustainable* signifies a holistic approach to winemaking that respects the ecosystem and surrounding society. But a sustainable wine isn't always organic. The term *organic* means produced without chemicals and pesticides and is applicable to the way the grapes were grown. Almost all finished products today cannot be labeled *organic* because they contain natural sulfites. These natural derivatives of the winemaking process keep wine fresh for decades. Only a tiny percentage of people are officially allergic to sulfites, and the organic label for wine carries a very high standard, with fewer than 10 parts per million of sulfites. Therefore, the label "made with organically grown grapes" is as close

> *Wine is constant proof that God loves us and loves to see us happy.*
>
> Benjamin Franklin, founding father and inventor

to "organic" as you're likely to find in a good bottle of wine. Notable exceptions include Frey Vineyards in Mendocino County, which guarantees USDA-labeled "sulfite-free" wine. Regardless of the degree of "greenness," any winemaker that is headed down the sustainability path is taking a step in the right direction.

Michael Honig is one of these vintners. Michael, who sits on the board of directors for the Wine Institute, is taking the institute's Sustainable Winegrowing Program to the next level by establishing a certification to offer over 1,100 wineries and related businesses a road map for going green. The Sustainable Winegrowing Program helps wine producers establish eco-friendly practices from ground to glass by developing guidelines and training to promote alternative energy, ecosystem management, composting, recycling, water conservation, and philanthropy. Through this effort, Michael is helping elevate the prestige of the entire region in the global wine market.

Touring us through Honig Vineyards, Michael pointed out sustainable features like a solar array; biodiesel in the trucks; a tributary restored by native vegetation; and ground-cover plants such as mustard seed, clover, and barley, which act as a natural blanket to cover the soil with organic matter. Honig also uses specially trained golden retrievers, known as "sniffer dogs," to detect the mealybug, an invasive species that first appeared in Southern California a decade ago. Sniffer dogs allow the wine grower to zero in on individual vines for removal, alleviating any broad use of pesticides.

Michael stopped at a box that looked like a birdhouse. "One of the ways we keep from using pesticides is by using bird boxes. Bluebirds eat an enormous amount of insects. To keep the insect and rodent population in check, we use hawk perches, barn owl boxes, bluebird boxes, and bat boxes." Using nature's resources to address the problem of insects sounded like a stroke of genius until I reminded myself that

Sustainable Wines and Vineyards

Here are some California vineyards known for being
solar-powered, organic, biodynamic, and/or otherwise sustainable:

Napa Valley, California

Araujo Estate Wines—www.araujoestatewines.com
Frog's Leap—www.frogsleap.com
Grgich Hills Estate—www.grgich.com
Hall Wines—www.hallwines.com
Honig Vineyard and Winery—www.honigwine.com
Joseph Phelps Vineyards—www.jpvwines.com
Miner Family Vineyards—www.minerwines.com
Robert Sinskey Vineyards—www.robertsinskey.com
Shafer—www.shafervineyards.com

Sonoma County, California

Benziger Winery—www.benziger.com
Cline Cellars—www.clinecellars.com
DeLoach Vineyards—www.deloachvineyards.com
Ferrari-Carrano—www.ferrari-carrano.com
Medlock Ames—www.medlockames.com
Red Truck Wines—www.redtruckwine.com
Ridge Vineyards—www.ridge.com

Mendocino County, California

Frey (America's first organic winery and the first maker of certified
biodynamic wines in the United States)—www.freywine.com
Parducci (first carbon-neutral winery in the United States)—
www.mendocinowinecompany.com

Other Resources

California Certified Organic Farmers—www.ccof.org
California Sustainable Winegrowing Alliance—www.
sustainablewinegrowing.org
Sonoma County Winegrape Commission—www.sonomawinegrape.org
Wine Institute—www.wineinstitute.org[10]

this was not an innovation, but simply the way it was meant to be.

The difference between sustainable vineyard owners and everyone else is that they see a tangible benefit to their bottom line by working in concert with nature. Since vineyards are farms, land is their natural capital; to preserve the health of the land is a long-term investment. "Is conservation the right thing to do? Absolutely. But green practices at Honig are integral to our business because they help us run a more efficient operation and help us produce a better product," Michael says. Honig's critically acclaimed wines are a testament to this fact.

Michael's strategic and pragmatic brand of sustainability has appeal for executives from other industries too. Honig has appeared in the *Wall Street Journal,* and Michael now finds himself inspiring companies in other industries to consider sustainability by giving speeches around the country. "We believe in leading by example," he says. "Our goal is to become one of the greenest wineries in the world."

Another leader in sustainability is DeLoach Vineyards, a certified organic winery known for its high-quality yet affordable wines and biodynamic farming, a "beyond organic" approach that ensures that the growth of a fruit or vegetable is in tune with the larger environment. The vineyard is located in nearby Sonoma County in the Russian River Valley, which wine experts consider "America's Burgundy" for producing the best Pinot Noir in the country. *Wine Enthusiast* magazine named owner Jean-Charles Boisset "Innovator of the Year" for 2008. I asked General Manager Lisa Heisinger to explain why. "Well, Boisset has a long history with sustainable viticulture," she said, "but I think the area in which we've provided leadership as a company is in sustainable packaging."

Lisa presented several of Boisset's greener innovations: wine in a plastic bottle embossed with a geometric design; wine in a lightweight aluminum bottle that chills rapidly; and a half-liter of wine in a recyclable cardboard container called Tetra Pak, a packaging that, when combined with ultra-high-temperature processing, allows liquid food to be packaged and stored at room temperature conditions for up to a year. This means perishable goods can be saved and distributed over greater distances without the need for energy-consuming refrigeration. These packaging alternatives are less energy-intensive than heavy glass bottles. They also require far less transportation.

This attentiveness to green packaging is not a marketing initiative but a company policy called the Boisset 70 Percent Rule. "More than 31.2 billion bottles of wine are consumed on earth each year," owner Jean-Charles Boisset says. "Seventy percent of that wine retails for less than $10 per bottle. Within that 70 percent, at least 70 percent is consumed between 28 minutes and 3 hours of purchase. Seventy percent of the cost of that wine is the packaging (bottles, corks, capsules, and all other dry goods), shipping, and other related supply-chain costs. The vast majority of the environmental impact of wine comes from the production and disposal of the packaging and from shipping the heavy merchandise around the world. We know that wine meant to be enjoyed young can be kept fresh and flavorful in a variety of packaging formats. Why not offer this wine in lighter, more environmentally friendly packaging that will reduce its carbon footprint and cost less to ship, yet still provide the high quality that customers demand?"

I asked Lisa when she thought Americans would come around on greener packaging for wine. "The wine market in America may well change because of the millennial generation," she said. "They are used to choices and adventure. We call it the Starbucks effect. Our grandparents just ordered coffee; today we choose from thirty different menu items at the coffee shop." She went on to explain, "One of the big things that woke us up was the success of Yellow Tail. The brand is affordably priced and fun. A whole new array of brands arose from this. We call them 'critter brands.' They are playful and fly in the face of the historical snobbish French-wine tradition."[11]

As consumers develop a taste for more "playfulness" in wines, a willingness to accept eco-friendly packaging may be next. For my part, I love Boisset's innovations now that I understand their purpose. And upon returning from my trip to California, I found Boisset's French Rabbit wine in eco-friendly cardboard containers on sale at Target. Thinking that Target's customers didn't understand the gems they were passing up, I took the opportunity myself to stock up on this eco-friendly quality wine at a great price.

While greener packaging is an important step, it is just one potential area of focus for a vintner who considers himself sustainable. There is no "one size fits all" approach that will be profitable for everyone. And, as Michael Honig quipped, "Sustainability also means 'sustaining your business.'" Since the most important feature of wine is its taste, organic practices would be worth little to the wine industry if they didn't actually enhance the product's quality. And quality is what we tasted on our sustainable wine tour. We sampled Pinot Noir, in which "ripe raspberries lift from the glass with aromas of strawberry-rhubarb tart," and Zinfandel, in which "violet perfume mingles with soft hints of barrel spice and walnut." Well, those were the descriptions we heard while tasting. We'll have to practice more to fully appreciate the subtleties. All I can say with assurance is that these wines tasted good!

The Beauty of Local

While tasting wines at DeLoach Vineyards, we dined on food prepared from their garden of over sixty varieties of vegetables and herbs, which is adjoined to a small farm with chickens, sheep, and pigs. Like the wines, the farm and gardens are tended according to a biodynamic philosophy. Mike and I were bowled over by the taste of our carrot–red lentil soup seasoned with cumin, curry, coriander, and ginger; the winter onion tartlet made with farm-fresh eggs and thick bacon; the organic herb salad; and a scrumptious trio of cheeses made with milk from goats, sheep, and cows. The delicious, delicate flavors of the locally and organically grown food transformed the simple menu into haute cuisine.

Back in Dallas I told my friend Julie about our experience. "I know what you mean," she said. "We just joined an organic produce co-op, and eating the vegetables is such a treat. I don't think it's my imagination that they just taste better."

Julie and I are having the same awakening that others across America are experiencing: where eating well is concerned, natural prevails over progress any day of the week. Enjoying good food with friends and family is a big part of living the good life. What a relief it is to know that it can be the best part of living the green life too.

Going Local

Locavore was the 2007 word of the year for the Oxford American Dictionary. Locavores, a group of "concerned culinary adventurers," formed in the Bay Area in 2005. Challenging themselves to eat food sourced within a 100-mile radius for one month, they sparked a worldwide movement.

For more information, visit www.locavores.com.

7

Eco-Chic Cars, Clothes, and Other Essentials

Fashion is not something that exists in dresses only. Fashion is in the sky, in the street, fashion has to do with ideas, the way we live, what is happening.

Coco Chanel, French designer, entrepreneur, and fashion icon

At some point in our quest to save, salvage, and conserve, most of us are going to break down and buy something. And that's not necessarily a bad thing. Seventy percent of the GDP in America is consumer driven, so shoppers actually help keep the economy going.[1] Unfortunately, most of us have kept it going on credit. Savvy green consumers practice conservation first. When you exercise the green advantage, you'll end up with more discretionary income. When it comes time to splurge, you have a choice to make. Will you perpetuate the problem or be the change?

I admit it. I love to buy nice things. I was glad to discover that I could channel the impulse into purchases that make a positive impact. Today we can find cars, clothes, computers, and other cool gadgets that take a bite out of climate change without breaking the bank. At the same time, we needn't get so hung up on fancy green labels that we forget the intrinsic value of quality craftsmanship, classic styling, and timeless design. Being a green consumer matters little unless we shift our mentality from disposability to longevity. By learning some basic shopping principles, we can comfortably consume without compromising our green credibility.

What Is a Green Product, Anyway?

Just for fun, imagine a product as a living creature: created from organic matter by an intelligent designer, born with a purpose, living a long and productive life, and returning to the earth upon its death. That is what a truly green product looks like. Unfortunately, most products are made with unintelligent design by inefficient factories and processes. (More than 90 percent of materials extracted to make durable goods become waste during production.) Many products have no real purpose, and at the end of their short lives, most are thoughtlessly discarded after little use. Landfills—aka graves for old furniture, carpets, clothes, televisions, shoes, computers, plastics, and organic materials such as diapers, paper, wood, and food wastes— hold billions of dollars' worth of material assets. What a waste!

What if we could reinvent industry to replace conventional products with ones so good that they become part of nature itself? We're almost there, according to William McDonough, world-renowned architect and notable green designer. "Wouldn't it be wonderful if, rather than bemoaning human industry, we had reason to champion it? If environmentalists as well as automobile makers could applaud every time someone exchanged an old car for a new one, because new cars purified the air and produced drinking water?"[2] In their book *Cradle to Cradle*, coauthors McDonough and Michael Braungart describe how eco-intelligent designs are being applied to buildings, systems, and products all over the world. "Ideally, cradle to cradle will become the mantra for product design. No company will enter a product development process without using these criteria," McDonough says.[3]

Several Popular Certifications for Consumer Products

A number of certifications exist to help eco-savvy consumers expedite their shopping. Below are just a few. Visit the websites for full details.

ENERGY STAR (www.energystar.gov)

- This was established to standardize energy efficiency for a range of products and buildings.
- It is continuously updated and is one of the most successful federal government programs.
- It applies to electronics, appliances, HVAC, and building systems.

Forest Stewardship Council (www.fsc.org)

- This is an independent, nonprofit organization that sets standards for sustainable forest management and accredits third-party organizations to certify products.
- It is the only sustainable wood certification recognized by the USGBC's LEED rating program and has wide industry recognition.
- It applies to forest and paper products.

Green-e (www.green-e.org)

- The Green-e logo means that an independent third party certified that the product meets strict consumer-protection and environmental standards.
- Products that display this logo have been manufactured using certified renewable energy or carbon offsets.
- It applies to retail electricity products using renewable energy; it can also apply to a range of consumer products made with renewable energy endorsed by Green-e.

A brilliant speaker and gifted designer, McDonough paints a vision of infinite possibilities for eco-friendly solutions. In reality, companies have been slow to adopt the cradle-to-cradle (C2C) certification. It has been applied to over 160 products, but this falls short of the goal of 30,000 certifications by 2012. Feasibility and affordability are several roadblocks that prevent manufacturers from adhering to McDonough's criteria.

Quite simply, there is no magic bullet, no single solution, and no "guru of green" that can forge a sustainable society for us. We are going to have to take this one step at a time, and it's going to require something from each of us. As we become more environmentally aware, products advertised as green will multiply and move mainstream. As long as products are manufactured and create waste, either in the process or at the end of their life, they can't be considered completely clean or green. For now, independent third-party certification offers the next best thing: transparency (corporate lingo for "honesty"). That part is up to manufacturers. Our job is to educate ourselves about the companies we buy from and the organizations that certify them.

Before we go into the best products your green can buy, let me share seven criteria I use to determine a product's green potential:

1. **Clean.** It emits the least amount of pollution possible for its category.
2. **Energy efficient.** Energy is not wasted in producing or operating the product.
3. **Water conscious.** Water is not wasted in manufacturing, and/or the product itself is a water-saving device.
4. **Recyclable.** At the end of its life, some or all of the product's parts can be recycled. This also goes for the packaging.

5. **Fair.** The environment is half the battle. People matter too! Are the workers who make the product compensated fairly? Are their working conditions safe?

6. **Certified.** Third-party certification validates the manufacturer's claims.

7. **Necessary.** No product can be green if you can easily do without it.

This list of criteria offers a straightforward and pragmatic way to evaluate purchases. Most products will not meet all seven criteria. We have to accept some trade-offs at least some of the time.

Green Cars

Here in Texas, cars are a fact of life—and the bigger the better. That is why Fort Worth seems an unlikely town for a green dealership to flourish. But despite the odds, EV-CARCO is pursuing their plans to build the nation's first coast-to-coast network of green car dealerships featuring the widest selection of alternative-fuel and hybrid cars under a single roof. EVCARCO is succeeding by catering to green consumers of every kind. Their executive team has done their homework to source the safest, most affordable, and most reliable vehicles available on the national and international markets.

"When I first started down this path, I was thinking primarily of profits. It's a business, after all. But this isn't just selling cars for me anymore," says CEO Dale Long, a former aviator in the US Army.

Good Guide uses a mountain of data to judge over 70,000 products and their social and environmental impact. Ratings are on a scale of 0 to 10, with 10 as the lowest impact. Sites such as Good Guide use a method called life-cycle assessment (LCA) to evaluate variables ranging from toxicity to working conditions in the manufacturing of products.

Visit www.goodguide.com to see how your favorite products are rated.

"It's bringing to market viable solutions to America's oil and environmental problems. Ultimately we want to offer the cleanest cars available at the best prices." The cleanest cars currently available are 100 percent electric vehicles (EVs), which plug into the wall and charge overnight, generally taking six to eight hours. One can buy an electric vehicle that costs between $8,000 and $17,000 after deducting a federal tax credit. "It will only cost you between $200 and $400 a year in electricity to drive. Also, you won't have to deal with the hassle or expense of oil changes and other maintenance," Dale says.

CEO Dale Long's Favorite EV Manufacturers

EnVision Motors—www.evcarco.com
Green Vehicles—
www.greenvehicles.com
Kandi—www.evcarco.com
Sunmotor Group LLC—
www.sunmotor.us
Tazzari—www.tazzari-zero.com
Wheego—www.wheego.net

Federal laws still keep most of these cars from going more than 25 to 35 miles per hour, depending on the state, so electric vehicle manufacturers tend to position these cars as "neighborhood vehicles." After test-driving one neighborhood vehicle, I can see them being quite reasonable for families needing a second car just for running errands.

In August 2009, major manufacturers began releasing information about the production of electric cars suitable for highway driving. GM announced that its Volt, the first mass-produced vehicle to claim more than 100 mpg composite fuel economy, is scheduled to start production in late 2010 as a 2011 model. The Volt is expected to travel up to 40 miles on electricity from a single battery charge and extend its overall range to more than 300 miles with its flex fuel-powered engine generator. The Renault-Nissan Alliance also announced its new EV called Leaf, due to be launched this year. The Leaf has a range of 100 miles and seats five adults. Ford, Toyota, Honda, Mercedes, BMW, and Mitsubishi have also released EV development news. With the introduction of more highway-speed vehicles, as well as innovations in batteries and charging infrastructure, 2010 will go down in history as the year the EV industry took a giant leap forward.

If you aren't ready for a full-on electric vehicle but want to do right by the environment, you have plenty of options with mainstream manufacturers. This year, battery technology advances will make hybrid vehicles at least twice as efficient as their predecessors and less expensive relative to inflation. The "third generation" 2010 Prius, which gives you a remarkable 51 mpg in the city and 48 mpg on the highway, starts at $22,000. A close second is the Honda Insight, averaging 40 mpg in the city and 43 mpg on the highway, and starting at around $19,800. For a luxury hybrid experience, try the 2010 Lexus RX 450h, which gets an impressive combined (city and highway) mileage of 37. It's also a Super Ultra Low Emission Vehicle (one of the cleanest of the California designations).

For an American-made hybrid that is packed with style, try the 2010 Ford Fusion Hybrid, which gets 41 mpg in the city and 36 mpg on the highway. Taking the automotive press by surprise, this car ranks at number 1 out of 24 affordable midsize cars. *USA Today* calls it "the best gasoline-electric hybrid yet." The review goes on to say, "It's so well-done

Top Hybrid SUVs for 2010

Want to do your part for the planet without sacrificing space, style, or comfort? Take a look at this range of choices:[4]

Make and Model	MPG City/Hwy	Base MSRP
Cadillac Escalade	20/21	$73,425
Chevrolet Tahoe	21/22	$50,455
Ford Escape	34/31	$31,500
GMC Denali Hybrid	21/22	$58,235
GMC Yukon Hybrid	21/22	$50,920
Lexus RX 450h	28/26	$42,111
Mercury Mariner	34/31	$30,090
Toyota Highlander	27/25	$34,700

that you have to look to the $107,000 Lexus LS 600h hybrid to come close."[5] By contrast, the Ford Fusion Hybrid carries a base MSRP of $27,270. My friend Reagan, who owns a new one, insisted I sit in hers to sample the leather-appointed interior. "Look at the dashboard," she said with excitement. "These little green leaves light up every time you shift into electric mode!" Reagan said the car actually inspires her to drive better.

Ford's combination of a hyper-efficient system, affordable luxury, and driver-friendly accessories proves that American car manufacturers are capable of producing innovations and good design at a reasonable price. According to a writer from the *Washington Post*, "After a week in the oh-so-smooth, technologically transparent Fusion Hybrid, I've not only become more of a believer in hybrids, but I've also moved closer than ever to buying a hybrid automobile. . . . I really like this car, mostly because it feels and looks like a nice, high-quality, midsize family sedan instead of a science project."[6]

EPA Green Vehicle Guide

For a hype-free resource, try EPA's new and improved Green Vehicle Guide. When researching your next vehicle purchase, use the Green Vehicle Guide to identify the cleanest, most fuel-efficient vehicles available. Each vehicle listed in the Green Vehicle Guide receives an air pollution score and a greenhouse gas score, on a scale of 1 to 10. No matter what size car, SUV, or pickup you need, you have greener options.

For more information, visit www.epa.gov/greenvehicles/Index.do.

Buying a used hybrid is a great way to drive a "recycled" low-emissions vehicle. "Most of the technology we're seeing out there is just a bridge to something better," Dale Long explains. "At EVCARCO, we strive to help customers find the very best vehicle for their budget and their circumstances. In many cases, a pre-owned model is the best fit." Dale adds, "All of these technologies are in transition. In another ten years everything will look different."

The key to being a greener driver is to evaluate the most environmentally sensitive options in your price range in terms of other concerns, such as your average travel distance and safety requirements. At the time of publication of this book, I'm still driving my 1998 Toyota 4Runner. It's fully paid off, and I mainly use it to drive the kids back and forth and run errands in my neighborhood. It doesn't make sense for me to run out and buy a new hybrid to prove I'm green when I am conserving energy by working from a LEED-certified home. When it comes time to replace my car, I'll have the great options already available as well as the technology on the horizon. For now I have my eyes on the Jeep Wrangler EV, one of Chrysler's concept cars. So, until I'm ready to buy again, I do what I can to keep my car in good condition, which helps save money and air quality. You can too. Visit www.fueleconomy.gov for tips and potential savings on all areas of car maintenance.

Green Clothes

Good news, ladies. "Eco-chic" fashion has come a long way from hemp wear that looks like a burlap sack. Today, retailers

151

are increasingly offering stylish green clothing options, but you still have to do a little digging. In general, eco-friendly clothes are still not widely available, the selection is limited, and the prices tend to be higher. I may be bullish on green, but I refuse to pay $300 for an "eco-friendly hoodie" from Barney's just to prove it.

Fortunately, some forward-thinking designers are working to make green clothes more readily available and offer them at reasonable prices. One of them is Debora Annino with Greenology USA. "We saw the opportunity for everyday casual lifestyle apparel, from jeans to jackets, tees to sweaters—a full collection to complement the American lifestyle," Debora told me. "Patagonia is a leader in eco-conscious outdoor-active wear, and you do see organic jeans and eco-fashion from high-end designers such as Loomstate and Stella McCartney. There haven't been more because this is really just becoming part of the mainstream." Debora continues, "We're seeing a growing interest from women who want better choices and products for their families—products that are natural, organic, and chemical free, such as infant and children's wear, bedding, and home textiles. They are starting to turn this thinking toward themselves. People are becoming more educated, and this is translating into increased demand."

As long as the prices are comparable, Debora believes people will make the better choice. To date, her company Greenology USA has created and produced organic and responsibly manufactured products for Belk's Madison Live Green brand, as well as developed green apparel for other brands. "Our company will continue to bring green product innovation to the apparel market," Debora said. "We are poising ourselves for the right time to make a dynamic presence with an affordable, accessible, fashionable, and conscientious brand that people can embrace without emptying their wallets."

Doug Newton, CEO of Real American Brands, Inc., is also on a mission to bring more green clothing options to mainstream shoppers. Over thirty years ago, Newton founded Billy Martin's, an upscale Western-lifestyle boutique, now located in Trump Plaza in New York City. Billy Martin's has amassed fans such as Sheryl Crow, Eric Clapton, Robin Williams, Don and Deirdre Imus, Dwight Yoakam, and Arnold Schwarzenegger. Newton recently added a federally registered trademark for Green Blues, a new denim apparel brand emphasizing eco-friendliness, fashion, and fit. Set to launch in 2010, Green Blues "is a logical next step for a company founded on the ideal of celebrating the best in America," according to Newton.

I asked Doug what inspired him to go in this direction. "I think the really good news is that, in America and hopefully other places around the world, we're seeing a change in the outlook and philosophy of consumers," he said. "People are increasingly thinking beyond themselves to embrace the needs of others and the planet we all share. Fashion, which is all about self-expression, is one of the best ways for a person to literally wear their convictions."

Not just for Hollywood elites, the green fashion wave is filtering into other markets. Payless Shoes, for example, recently launched zoe&zac, a new line

Green Fashions at Any Price!

Green clothing used to fall into two categories: camping gear and high-end luxury apparel. Now designers are creating eco-friendly fashions that appeal to shoppers across the spectrum:

"Eco-luxe"

Bahar Shahpar—
www.baharshahpar.com
Linda Loudermilk—
www.lindaloudermilk.com
The Battalion—www.thebattalion.us

"Eco-affordable"

Deborah Lindquist—
www.deborahlindquist.com
Eco Skin—www.ecoskincollections.com
Eileen Fisher—www.eileenfisher.com
Loomstate—www.loomstate.com
Threads for Thought—www.
threadsforthought.com

"Eco-economical"

Blue Canoe—www.bluecanoe.com
Jonäno—www.jonano.com
Patagonia—www.patagonia.com
REI—www.rei.com
zoe&zac—www.payless.com

of affordable, stylish, and eco-friendly shoes and accessories. All items are priced below $30 and packaged in 100 percent recycled boxes printed with soy-based inks. Offering hip designs crafted from eco-friendly materials such as organic cotton and linen, natural hemp, jute, recycled rubber, and water-based glues, the line "democratizes" green fashion by making it affordable and accessible.

Large mid-tier retailers such as Kohl's are catching the sustainability wave too. Even so, the market is not exactly flooded with a fantastic selection of high-quality, afford-able green products. Jim Thomas, the vice president of corporate social responsibility at JCPenney, explained why eco-fashions are hard to find: "Among mainstream retail-ers, this is a slow process, although it is steadily moving forward. JCPenney is no exception." While it doesn't stock a plethora of green products, JCPenney does demonstrate exceptional leadership in terms of reducing its carbon footprint. It has been the recipient of the EPA's ENERGY STAR Partner of the Year Award for three different years, earning the prestigious Sustained Excellence Award in 2009. JCPenney is the first retailer to be so honored for its efforts in using energy efficiency in facility operations and integrating superior energy management into overall organizational strategy.

In order to remain competitive, retailers such as JCPenney must select inventory based on margins and volume rather than innovation and environmental altruism. "Our customers aren't as willing to pay a premium. So we're demonstrating environmental responsibility in some other ways," Jim said. "We sell cloth bags for $1.99 to encourage our customers to reduce their waste. We've sold over 400,000 since we launched them last year in our stores." What about operations? "The plastic, cardboard, and hangers from our stores are consoli-dated at our seventeen different logistics centers. Last year we recycled 93,500 tons of cardboard, 4,400 tons of plastic, and 165 million hangers. Lined up, the hangers would go around the globe one and two-thirds times!" Jim also said that more than 800 of over 1,000 stores have designated Energy Captains, people at each site whose responsibility it is to implement green programs. The retailer is working with managers and associates to equip them with tools to run their own green teams.

To take steps toward offering greener products, JCPenney created its own product category, "Simply Green." JCPenney uses it primarily for its private-label products but also extends the privilege to interested suppliers. When one of the nation's largest retailers of clothing helps suppliers implement processes to conserve energy or water and encourages the use of recycled content, it has a sizable impact on the industry. One notable example is Levi's. According to Michael Kobori, Levi's vice president for Supply Chain Social and Environmental Sustainability, a study found that one pair of 501 jeans consumed 918 gallons of water in its life cycle. "This water includes everything from growing the cotton that's used to make the jeans to the number of times it goes in the washing machine," Kobori said. "The water we use is one of our most significant impacts on the environment, and we saw we had to reduce our footprint." Levi's has taken measures to do so, including working with retailers such as JCPenney, who was the first major chain to carry Levi's Eco jeans made from 100 percent organic cotton.

Urban Cowboy

Start greening your closet with a pair of new jeans. Here are several eco-friendly denim brands to choose from:

Canyon River Blues (men's)—$42 (www.sears.com)
Edun (various styles)—$85 to $235 (www.edunonline.com)
Good Society Slim Leg Jeans— $99 (www.tobi.com)
Joe's Jeans (various styles)—$158 to $168 (www.joesjeans.com)
Levi's Eco Jeans (various styles) —$68 to $78 (www.levis.com)
Loomstate Flux State—$89 (www.loomstate.org)

I asked Jim Thomas why this kind of leadership hasn't translated into more green products on the shelves. "Our primary value proposition is style and quality at a smart price," Jim said. "So what I try to do is focus on style and quality at a smart price with a reduced environmental impact. If we can get that, we've got a home run. The challenge right now is that reduced environmental impact directly translates into price. Organic cotton costs 10 to 20 percent more than conventional cotton. Recycled polyester is more expensive than virgin material. Our research tells us that our customers aren't willing to pay much

Eco-Chic Wardrobe Summary

The power we hold as consumers is significant. We can help drive demand by sharing our enthusiasm for greener options with our favorite retailers. In the meantime, we can also make smarter, more sustainable decisions (and still look great!) by following these tips:

1. **Cancel your catalogs.** Catalog Choice (www.catalogchoice.org) is a free service that allows you to reduce your mailbox clutter while helping save natural resources. You'll also save money by not indulging in all those spontaneous purchases.
2. **Buy quality.** My nicest handbags have lasted me a decade.
3. **Build your base out of classic styles.** The little black dress never goes out of style. Neither will most coats, jackets, boots, scarves, sundresses, and suits.
4. **Limit trendy purchases to three per season.** Save yourself some money. Many of these items won't be in style within two years. Two new tops and a pair of shoes will go a long way.
5. **Ease into eco-apparel.** Start with organic cotton body wear and T-shirts.
6. **Keep it casual.** Increase your comfort level, minimize dry cleaning, and save money.
7. **Get creative with eco-accessories.** Have fun (and feel young!) with a purse made from salvaged candy wrappers or necklaces made with recycled Coke cans and Scrabble pieces. Find handmade accessories such as these at www.trendyshoppes.com and www.etsy.com.
8. **Go vintage.** You can enjoy quality, high-end designs and recycle at the same time. Why buy an energy-intensive knockoff when you can still find the real thing? Vintage accessories will help you cultivate a personal style that others will appreciate but no one can imitate.

more for green. But everything else being equal, they would prefer green products. Green is a great tiebreaker."

Green Computers

The global IT industry accounts for 2 percent of the world's carbon emissions—the carbon-footprint equivalent of the airline industry. Thanks in part to pressure from nonprofits like Greenpeace International (www.greenpeace.org), which has published quarterly versions of its landmark "Guide to Greener Electronics" since 2006, computer manufacturers now understand that consumers care about the environmental footprints of the products they use. The latest version of Greenpeace's guide shows that most electronics companies are not making the changes necessary to significantly cut carbon emissions. Of all the companies surveyed, only Fujitsu, Philips, and Sharp support the cuts in pollution levels necessary to reach a 2020 target of cutting emissions by 30 percent in industrial countries. Additionally, only HP and Philips have committed to substantial cuts in their own emissions.

The electronics companies also had low scores in the usage of renewable energy, with only Nokia achieving the 25 percent clean power mark. So while surveyed companies have made strides in reducing toxic chemicals in their products—all Apple products were free of PVC and brominated flame retardants by the end of 2008—there is still much progress to be made in the electronics industry.

When shopping for your next computer, here are a few simple rules to follow. First, investigate the sustainability programs of manufacturers to see what they are doing to protect the planet. Second, ask about the use of recycled materials in product development and what the manufacturer offers in the way of recycling. Third, buy a laptop, which saves 50 to 80 percent energy over a desktop. Visit EPEAT (www.epeat. net) for a free online guide to help you evaluate and compare electronic products based on their environmental attributes.

PC magazine assessed dozens of personal computers according to environmental standards it developed in-house based on energy efficiency, recyclability, and the toxicity of components. The publication also factored in various green certifications such as EPA's ENERGY STAR program, the European Union's Restriction of Hazardous Substances directive, Taiwan's Greenmark, and the computer industry's own Electronic Products Environmental Assessment Tool.

Their top choices for greener desktop computers are:

Apple's Mac Mini
Zonbu's Desktop Mini
HP Compaq's 2710p and dc7800
Lenovo's ThinkCentre a61e
Dell's OptiPlex 755
    The greenest laptop models include:
Dell's Latitude D630
Everex Zonbu
Fujitsu's LifeBook S6510
Toshiba's Tecra A9-S9013

Even though they aren't a front-runner in the reduction of carbon emissions, I admit that I am partial to Apple because of their philosophy of in-store education. Getting customer service is indispensable to me as a small business owner. In early 2009 I purchased the aluminum 13-inch MacBook, an ENERGY STAR–qualified laptop with a highly recyclable aluminum and glass outer shell. (Recyclability is one area that has improved quite a lot in the industry.) The company keeps paper to a minimum by using the website and in-store signage to communicate product information instead of glossy marketing materials. Apple also offers customers the option of receiving electronic receipts instead of paper.

Computers are a fact of life, and bringing down the carbon footprint of the IT industry is something we will have to continue wrestling with. And just as important as the greenness of your new computer is what you do with your old one. Putting it in the trash allows heavy metals and other toxins to migrate into surrounding soils and water. If the machine still works, give it to a local school that can put it to use, or to Goodwill or the Salvation Army, either of which can resell it to fund programs. Another option is to donate it to the National Cristina Foundation, which gives outdated technology to needy nonprofits.

Green Gadgets and Accessories

Green retailers of all stripes are springing up across America. Several ones I like include:

- Anna Sova (www.annasova.com), offering "the world's finest-quality certified organic cotton bedding and bath."
- Green Living (www.green-living.com), offering a dynamic selection of green gadgets, housewares, gifts, toys, and accessories. They have a wonderful selection of eco-friendly paint and green home decor.
- Lehman's (www.lehmans.com), offering hundreds of products for simple, self-sufficient living. This is an old-school approach to green steeped in tradition and quality. A number of items are handmade by the Amish.
- You can find many other green stores and services by viewing the National Green Pages at www.coopamerica .org/pubs/greenpages.

8

A Buyer's Guide to Toxin-Free Living

If a million of us spent just $1,000 on safer cosmetics and personal-care products, we'd have a $1 billion impact on this industry. That's not the kind of shopping "spree" any manufacturer can afford to ignore.

Diane MacEachern,
author of *Big Green Purse*

Sometimes we get so busy having a green party that we forget to step back and remember why it started. Long before the polar bear became its poster child, the green revolution began as a means of protecting people's health from hazards caused by big industry. In 1962, Rachel Carson launched the modern environmentalist movement with her famous book *Silent Spring*, in which she challenged the practices of agricultural scientists and the government, calling for a change in the way humankind viewed the natural world. Carson was attacked by the chemical industry and some in the government as an alarmist, but she courageously reminded us that we are vulnerable to the same damage as the rest of the ecosystem.

Today we are still relinquishing responsibility for our health to organizations with no vested interest in our well-being. The Food and Drug Administration (FDA) does not regulate cosmetics, personal-care products, or cleaning products, although evidence is mounting that these chemicals are contributing to asthma, the early onset of puberty in girls, the feminization of baby boys, reproductive and immune system deficiencies, breast cancer, and testicular cancer—one of the fastest growing cancers in the world.

While food and drink are obvious vehicles for ingesting chemicals into our bodies, our pores, noses, and eyes are as capable as our mouths of absorbing toxic substances. We should be no less vigilant in choosing our cosmetics and cleaning agents than we are in choosing our cuisine. Once we know what to look for, we can use our spending power to send a loud-and-clear message to manufacturers, encouraging them to stay accountable if they want to keep us as their customers.

Understanding the Science

Environmental scientist Theo Colborn was called "the Rachel Carson of the '90s" for coauthoring the 1996 groundbreaking work *Our Stolen Future*. As with Carson, some critics first dismissed Colborn's work as pseudoscientific and controversial. And just as Carson was proved to be right, so too was Colborn. Over a decade later, Colborn's findings have become common knowledge in the scientific community. In fact, those who are building on her work are finding that not only was Colborn right, but the problems she uncovered are even worse than she thought they were.

Using a multidisciplinary approach merging toxicology, endocrinology, embryology, and psychology, Colborn discovered a common cause to the wide-ranging effects of pollution on wildlife on virtually every corner of the earth. As she pored over hundreds of unrelated studies, her quest to uncover the causes of reproductive abnormalities in animals led her to discover the same problems in humans. Why did the rate of testicular cancer triple in Denmark between the 1940s and the 1980s? Why were human sperm that were studied under microscopes showing up deformed—some with two heads, others with two tails, and others with frenetic hyperactivity? How did the average male sperm count drop by almost 50 percent between 1938 and 1990 while testicular cancer jumped sharply in studies spanning the United States, Europe, India, Nigeria, Hong Kong, Thailand, Brazil, Libya, Peru, and Scandinavia?[1]

Amid her research Colborn discovered a central piece of the puzzle in the world of Frederick vom Saal, a biologist at the University of Missouri. In his studies on lab mice, vom Saal observed dramatic deviations in the sexual behavior of mice exposed to synthetic chemicals at key stages in their development. These chemicals, called endocrine disrupters, threw the hormonal balance of the subjects' bodies off-kilter.[2] Even though the experiments were performed on lab mice, these results are

Beauty Is Only Skin-Deep

A report titled "Skin Deep" by the Environmental Working Group (EWG), a nonprofit research institute based in Washington DC, showed that 89 percent of 10,500 ingredients used in personal-care products have not been evaluated for safety! The EWG also reports that more than 750 personal-care products sold in the United States violate industry safety standards or cosmetic safety standards in other industrialized markets such as Canada, Japan, and the European Union.

The EWG's Skin Deep database compares ingredients in more than 41,000 products against 50 definitive toxicity and regulatory databases, making it the largest integrated data resource of its kind. It is a free resource that can help you investigate your preferred products and find alternatives if necessary. Visit www.cosmeticsdatabase.com.

relevant to us. Scientists concur that hormones guide development in essentially the same way in all mammals.[3]

Given the evidence, it is appalling that the products we apply directly to our bodies and breathe in every day are not regulated. The industry claims to regulate itself, but most manufacturers do not even adhere to the FDA's requirement to put a warning statement on the front of products that have not been tested.[4]

The European Union and other international markets have stricter standards for the ingredients allowed in personal-care products. Why is this not the case in the United States? It comes down to a difference in philosophy. Industry-sponsored scientists explain that these chemicals do not pose a risk to humans in small doses. The problem with this rationale is that consumers do not use each of these products by themselves. A product-use survey of 2,300 men and women, conducted by the Environmental Working Group in 2004, showed that a quarter of all women and 1 of every 100 men used at least 15 products daily.[5]

Moreover, the degree of hormones' sensitivity to endocrine disrupters approaches the unfathomable; as vom Saal says, it is "beyond people's wildest imagination." The authors of *Our Stolen Future* explain hormone sensitivity this way:

> Hormones are exceptionally potent chemicals that operate at concentrations so low that they can be measured only by the most sensitive analytical methods. When considering hormones such as estradiol, the most potent estrogen, forget parts per million or parts per billion. The concentrations are typically parts per trillion, one thousand times *lower* than parts per billion. One can begin to imagine a quantity so infinitesimally small by thinking of a drop of gin in a train of tank cars full of tonic. One drop in 660 tank cars would be one part in a trillion; such a train would be six miles long.[6]

We must ask ourselves if an industry that places profit ahead of public health is really capable of regulating itself. For my part, I prefer to play it safe by buying alternative products, considering the potential consequences. On a sheer anecdotal level, three of my closest friends suffer from endometriosis, and a number of others have experienced problems conceiving. Coincidence? Not to Theo Colborn, who doesn't mince words: "What I've always said is that we are neutering the population."[7]

Red-Flag Ingredients

Now that I have your attention, let me share the good news. Even though we don't know everything there is to know, we have all the information we need to buy safe products today. And thanks to more companies getting a conscience, we have a wider selection to choose from and more stores offering them than ever before.

Before getting into which products to purchase, let's cover the ingredients to avoid. National Geographic's *Green Guide* is an excellent reference for consumers interested in a comprehensive explanation of the environmental and health-related effects of every action occurring in our daily lives. *The Green Guide* has compiled a list of the twelve most hazardous ingredients commonly found in personal-care products:[8]

1. **Antibacterials** common in hand soaps and deodorants wipe out the good bacteria that protect against germs like E. coli, salmonella, and staph. Ironically, children reared in an overly sterile environment experience more allergies, asthma, and eczema because the body's immune system does not get the opportunity to mature. In a healthy household, this level of "clean" is unnecessary and can do more harm than good.
2. **Coal tar** is an active ingredient and a known carcinogen in dandruff shampoos and anti-itch creams. Coal tar–based dyes such as **FD&C Blue 1** and **FD&C Green 3**,

used in toothpaste and mouthwash, have been found to cause cancer in animals.

3. **Diethanolamine (DEA)**, widely used in shampoos to increase lather, is a possible hormone disrupter and depletes the body of choline, an essential nutrient for cell functioning and development. Its compounds and derivatives are **triethanolamine (TEA)** and **monoethanolamine (MEA)**. DEA, TEA, and MEA can react to create nitrosamines, which cause cancer in lab mice.

4. **1,4-Dioxane** is a known animal carcinogen and probable human carcinogen that can appear in shampoo and body wash and other products containing **sodium laureth sulfate**. It also can be found in ingredients with the terms **"PEG," "-xynol," "ceteareth," "oleth,"** and most other ethoxylated (chemically altered) **"eth"** ingredients. A 2007 survey by the Campaign for Safe Cosmetics found traces of dioxane in dozens of children's bath products and adult personal-care products, and 15 percent of shampoos tested contained amounts above the FDA's suggested maximum of ten parts per million.

5. **Formaldehyde** causes immune-system toxicity, respiratory irritation, and cancer in humans. It is a common contaminant or breakdown product of **diazolidinyl urea, imidazolidinyl urea, bronopol**, and **quaternium** compounds in baby bath soap, nail polish, and hair dye.

6. **Fragrance**, a catchall term that permits manufacturers to keep their formulations a secret, can mask **phthalates**, which act as hormone disrupters and have been shown to cause birth and reproductive defects in lab animals.

7. **Lead** and **mercury** may appear in products as a naturally occurring contaminant of **hydrated silica**, an ingredient in toothpaste. Brain-damaging mercury, found in the preservative **thimerosal**, is used in some mascaras.

8. **Nanoparticles,** tiny particles of minerals intended to make products more blendable, can penetrate the skin and damage brain cells. Of most concern are nanoparticles of **zinc oxide** and **titanium dioxide,** used in sunscreens. When possible, look for sunscreens containing particles of those ingredients larger than 100 nanometers.

9. **Parabens** are common preservatives in many toiletries and may be listed on labels as **methyl-, ethyl-, propyl-, butyl-,** or **isobutylparaben.** Parabens mimic the hormone estrogen in the body, a process that has been linked to breast cancer, infertility, and endometriosis.

10. **Petroleum distillates** are possible human carcinogens and are prohibited for use in the European Union. They can still be found in several US brands of mascara, foot-odor powder, and other products. Watch for the terms **petroleum** and **liquid paraffin.**

11. **P-Phenylenediamine (PPD),** common in hair dyes, can damage the nervous system and cause lung irritation, allergic reactions, and blindness. It can also appear on labels as **1,4-Benzenediamine, p-Aminoaniline,** and **1,4-Diaminobenzene.**

12. **Hydroquinone** is found in skin and under-eye creams. It is neurotoxic and allergenic. There is some evidence that it may cause cancer in lab animals.

Take this opportunity to go through your cabinets and dispose of products that contain these red-flag ingredients. Next time you go shopping, replace your old products with safe and healthy alternatives. The best way to ensure the safety of the products you purchase is to get to know the companies behind them.

Terms such as "natural," "nontoxic," "cruelty-free," "eco-safe," "dermatologist-tested," "nature's friend," and "hypoallergenic" can mean little. The most credible labels are backed by third-party verification or seals. Manufacturers that are

Safer Personal-Care Product Manufacturers

Diane MacEachern's book *Big Green Purse* is an incredible resource to help you use your spending power to create a cleaner, greener world. Out of hundreds of cosmetic and personal-care product manufacturers, *Big Green Purse* selected the following as the best at limiting the number of toxic ingredients they use[9]:

Alima Cosmetics—www.alimacosmetics.com
Aubrey Organics—www.aubrey-organics.com
Burt's Bees—www.burtsbees.com
Dr. Bronner—www.drbronner.com
Ecco Bella—www.eccobella.com
Everyday Minerals—www.everydayminerals.com
Honeybee Gardens—www.honeybeegardens.com
Jason—www.jasonnatural.com
Miessence—www.miessenceproducts.com
The Organic Makeup Company—www.organicmakeup.ca
Pangea Organics—www.pangeaorganics.com
Terressentials—www.terressentials.com
Tom's of Maine—www.tomsofmaine.com
Vermont Soapworks—www.vermontsoap.com

serious about being green will substantiate their claims. At the very least, manufacturers should offer a transparent explanation of the product's ingredients.

What's Safe?

If you are looking for a store offering an extensive line of green personal-care products, Aveda will give you a complete green experience. The company has a solid corporate sustainability policy and decades of leadership. Aveda stores offer customers a spa-like shopping environment. Aveda's green branding and marketing is supported by substantive product innovations encased in eco-friendly packaging. I love my Aveda "environmental compact" made with recycled aluminum, which I frequently show clients as an example of clever eco-design. Another excellent company is Origins, which makes the only USDA-certified organic cosmetic line in the country. For a first-rate bathing experience, you can't do better than three squirts of Dr. Bronner's "Magic" Pure Castile Peppermint soap (available at Target, Whole Foods, and many other stores) in a hot bath. This soap contains organic oils and can be used for eighteen separate cleaning purposes. Mike and I also enjoy using Burt's Bees products. Burt's Bees offers an all-natural line of skin and hair care for men, women, and babies at affordable prices.

If you discover that your favorite products are not being manufactured to the highest safety and/or sustainability standards, urge the manufacturer to sign the Compact for Safe Cosmetics (www.safecosmetics.org), which involves companies that commit to comply with European Union standards by replacing 450 hazardous chemicals with safer, nontoxic alternatives.

Get Clean, Breathe Easy

In 2005 the Centers for Disease Control and Prevention found that the bodies of Americans age six and older are contaminated by an average of 148 specific toxic substances.[10] The sources of these toxins are the very products we use on our bodies and in our homes every day. When we realize that of the 80,000 chemicals listed with the EPA, only 20 percent have been tested, we can begin to see how toxins could so easily seep into our society.

If this news makes you want to stay inside, think again. According to the EPA, levels of organic pollutants are two to five times higher inside our homes than outside![11] When I first learned this, I felt completely helpless. I work from home and now that's not even safe? And how can I protect my four-year-old daughter and two-year-old son?

Dr. Alan Greene, an attending pediatrician at the Lucile Packard Children's Hospital at Stanford University School of

Medicine, looked at blood collected from babies at the moment of birth to see what they were exposed to, and he found an average of 200 industrial chemicals coursing through their bodies even before they were born. Those are things from the environment, modern chemicals that people never had to deal with in the past.[12]

There's no polite way of saying this: your body is a landfill, a dumping ground for a mind-boggling array of toxic chemicals. So is mine. So is your child's.

Sloan Barnett, consumer advocate

For the most part, we still don't know what this is doing to our kids. We do know that childhood diseases are on the rise. Childhood cancer rates jumped 26 percent between 1975 and 1998. The number of children in special education programs increased 191 percent from 1977 to 1994. Childhood asthma rates increased 100 percent between 1980 and 1995. While these rate increases could be the result of better diagnoses and reporting, they still indicate problems of epidemic proportions.[13]

Sloan Barnett, a consumer advocate and author of *Green Goes with Everything*, explains the correlation between these startling statistics and the cleaning products inside our own homes. "The most dangerous air pollution we face every day is indoors, right here inside our homes where most of us spend 90 percent of our time," Sloan says in her book. "Our homes can actually make us sick because they're filled with invisible poisons and toxic air. The stuff we use to wash our clothes and dishes, clean our teeth and floors, can shorten our lives."[14] Sloan is the wife of Roger Barnett, the CEO of Shaklee, but her role as an environmental spokesperson actually stems from her lifelong affinity for environmental causes, not to mention sheer maternal instinct.

The mother of three children, Sloan awakened to the dangers of environmental pollution when her son Spencer, at age three, suddenly couldn't breathe. Sloan and her husband rushed

5 Easy Steps to a Healthy Child and Healthy World

Nancy and James Chuda founded the Healthy Child, Healthy World organization after their five-year-old Colette died of a rare, nongenetic form of cancer. "Colette was our daughter. It is because of Colette—and the countless other children whose lives are being lost to cancer and other childhood diseases that are linked to hazards in the environment—that we are reaching out to you. We want to share with you what parents who have lost children tragically to cancer have learned, and what together we can do about this terrible threat to all children."[15]

Here are 5 ways you can protect your child's heath:

1. **Avoid using pesticides.** To prevent pest problems without using harsh chemicals, remove food sources from countertops. Block holes with caulk. Use welcome mats. Encourage clean shoes or shoe removal inside the house.
2. **Clean safely.** Use safer cleaning products. Fact sheets are available at www. healthychild.org.
3. **Help children breathe easier.** On a typical cleaning day, levels of pollutants inside can be hundreds and thousands of times higher than the outdoor air in the most polluted of cities. Always use the least toxic products. Open the windows. (Doing so for just five minutes a day can vastly improve indoor air quality.) Grow plants. Use a vacuum with a HEPA filter.
4. **Provide healthy food.** Buy foods with the least amount of contaminants. Provide low-fat dairy and meat to avoid exposure to toxins. Avoid prepackaged foods, which have added chemicals in food colorings and flavors.
5. **Use plastic products wisely.** Chemicals in plastics have been linked to cancers, birth defects, poor nervous systems, and hormone disruption in babies. Get rid of plastics that show wear and tear. Do not microwave foods in plastic containers. If you must use plastics, look for those labeled 1, 2, 4, or 5, or bio-based plastics made from natural ingredients such as corn.

Spencer to the hospital, where the doctors immediately placed him on oxygen and gave him steroids to clear his airways. "We spent the next two nights in the intensive care unit. . . . We were confused and sick with worry," Sloan writes. When the doctor told her it was asthma, Sloan was shocked. "Ultimately, we knew our son's condition had to be either genetic or environmental. Neither my husband nor I had any family history of asthma, going back for four generations. So we concluded the cause was environmental." A journalist, Sloan shifted into research mode and discovered she wasn't alone. One in thirteen school-age kids in the United States has asthma. "At least six well-designed epidemiological studies have found one answer: a strong link between the use of certain cleaning products and asthma," Sloan continues. "That stopped me cold. The cause of my son's asthma may have been me. I may have been poisoning my own son."[16] Sloan did what any of us would have done: she dived in headfirst to change her routine.

Several Safer Cleaning Product Manufacturers

Bi-O-Kleen—www.bi-o-kleen.com
Bon Ami—www.bonami.com
Citra-Solv—www.citra-solv.com
Earth Choice/OdoBan—www.odoban.com/MenuEarthChoice.html
Earth Friendly—www.ecos.com
Ecover—www.ecover.com/us/en
Method—www.methodhome.com
Mrs. Meyer's Clean Day—www.mrsmeyers.com
Seventh Generation—www.seventhgeneration.com
Shaklee—www.shaklee.net
Simple Green—www.simplegreen.com

I can relate. Although my home environment should have been a starting point, I have to admit that assessing my cleaning products was not first (or even second) on my list of things to do to save the world. As a big-picture person, smaller housekeeping items can fall through the cracks. But after becoming a mother, I developed a sense of responsibility to learn how to protect my kids from potential hazards. But where was I supposed to begin?

I have a good friend and neighbor to thank for patiently educating me on the merits of making safer cleaning products a mission-critical part of my green journey. Pam Hoffmann is the wife of our green builder, Alan. As a Shaklee distributor, Pam is more nutritionist than salesperson. Pam is great at what she does because her focus is helping people make healthier choices through education and information sharing.

When we moved into our new home, Pam gave me a Get Clean starter kit, containing a full supply of earth-friendly home-cleaning products and concentrates with refillable, recyclable containers. According to the company, when compared to the same quantity of ready-to-use cleaning products in conventional packaging, the Get Clean starter kit eliminates 108 pounds of packaging waste from landfills and 248 pounds of greenhouse gas.

Pam offered to show me how to use it, so I invited our housekeeper Alex to join us. Alex and his wife Lilian have cleaned our home twice a month for the past seven years. They had their system down pat, so I worried about getting them to switch. Pam said, "Alex, you are going to be excited to use these products because they are so much better for you. Being exposed to hazardous chemicals on a daily basis can really harm your health." After Pam spent half an hour educating us, Alex, a strapping man in his early thirties, told her, "I've been suffering from headaches and nosebleeds. I didn't realize how these chemicals could be hurting me."

I remembered that Alex wore a mask when he cleaned the bathtub, although he never complained. Suddenly my heart went out to him. Alex is a hardworking father who moved to America from Brazil in search of a better life. He and Lilian pushed themselves to the limits to build a cleaning business from scratch. In fact, Mike and I were among their very first customers. I was glad to see what Alex had accomplished, but it hadn't occurred to me that he was putting his life on the line to clean my bathtub.

Needless to say, Alex and Lilian didn't mind switching to the new products. I was glad to do it too, even though I secretly feared they wouldn't work as well. After two years of

Cleaning for a Cause

Greening the Cleaning is an award-winning product line created by Deirdre Imus, founder of the Deirdre Imus Environmental Center, a not-for-profit corporation at Hackensack University Medical Center. For the retail line, 100 percent of all after-tax profits from sales go to the Imus Cattle Ranch for Kids with Cancer.

For more information, visit www.dienviro.com and www.imusranchfoods.com.

use, I have not noticed a single area of my house that isn't at least as clean as before. Knowing it is healthier for the people who help me makes me love these products all the more.

As with personal-care products, a number of safe, affordable, and effective alternatives are on the market today. And if you want to get really serious about saving green while going green, try mixing your own. According to author David Bach, you can save $580 a year by making your own biodegradable cleaning products out of everyday ingredients such as baking soda, club soda, vinegar, and salt.[17]

The Dirt on Clean

Conventional cleaning products range from mildly irritating to downright deadly. What should you be looking for at the store? Here are a few tips from *The Green Guide*:

1. Products labeled **"Danger"** or **"Poison"** tend to be the most hazardous. Those marked "Warning" or "Caution" are moderately or slightly toxic. Also avoid labels such as "may cause skin irritation," "flammable," "vapors harmful," and "may cause burns on contact."

2. **Avoid** products that contain **chlorine** or **ammonia** as their main ingredients. They can cause respiratory and skin irritation and create toxic fumes if accidentally mixed together.

3. Labels such as "natural," "eco-friendly," and even "non-toxic" often mean nothing. Instead, look for "solvent-free," "plant-based," "no phosphates," and "no petroleum-based ingredients."[18]

Are You Hazardous Too?

When it comes to the state of the planet, we can't assign all the blame to chemicals and big industry; we also bear some of the responsibility. We need to become more educated consumers and better users of the products we purchase.

SustainLane.com, an online green-living community, is an amazing resource chock-full of green product reviews, articles, fun do-it-yourself ideas, recipes, and how-to advice. Visit www.sustainlane.com/directory for product reviews and green tips on topics ranging from bed and bath to banking and investing. You can find recipes for all-natural cleaning agents that you can mix with ingredients from your pantry. You can even find local city listings for stores offering clean and green products from L.A. and Albuquerque to Minneapolis and Philadelphia.

If research is not your thing, you can still get by on common sense. If a product is marked "dangerous" or "hazardous," it is! If your eyes water while walking down the cleaning aisle at the store, there's a good chance those chemicals will pollute your home's air too. Commit to purchasing the safest products available to you. Isn't your family's health worth it? Most of us will never have the power to force higher industry standards, but we all have the power to vote with our dollars.

9

Blueprint for a Green Remodel

> The green building movement needs to rethink
> its focus on fitting ever more energy-saving de-
> vices into increasingly goofy buildings. Archi-
> tecture that instead taps into public tastes for
> tradition, familiarity and comfort will give us
> places that create their own natural preserva-
> tion societies, because they are loved. Reusing
> old buildings is the true green architecture.
> Buildings designed for decades must give way
> to buildings designed for centuries.
>
> David Brussat,
> editor for *The Providence Journal*

In 2007 my family and I had a custom green home built. Our builder Alan Hoffmann worked with the US Green Building Council to qualify our house for LEED certification. In fact, it earned a platinum rating, the highest available. By all standards our home is sustainable (that is, until you compare it to a mud hut in Africa, a yurt in Mongolia, or an adobe Pueblo village). As with most everything else, the term *green* is relative. I love our house and would recommend the ICF (insulated concrete form) mode of construction to anyone who aims to build for maximum efficiency, comfort, and longevity. However, if we're going to really talk sustainability, we have to look at solutions that are accessible, affordable, and desirable to everyone.

We live in an urban neighborhood where houses range from brand-new to run-down. If you drive down my street, you'll see a number of frame houses built in the 1940s and 1950s. In some cases these lovingly renovated bungalows, painted in fresh colors and surrounded by manicured gardens, become more charming with age and patina. In other cases the houses are downright dilapidated. Well-cared-for or not, almost all of these houses are eight times less efficient than my concrete house. But then some of my neighbors think my home is too big, too new, and too expensive. So there's the rub. Not everybody is going to spring for green construction. Some think they can't pay the extra 4 to 8 percent that sustainable construction can cost (although the costs pay for themselves). Others may prefer the charm of an antique home. And in the wake of the mortgage-lending crisis, many others don't have the option to move. For all these reasons, this chapter advises on green-home remodeling, not green-home building.

> *He is the happiest, be he king or peasant, who finds peace in his home.*
>
> Johann Wolfgang von Goethe, German poet and natural philosopher

But there is still one more reason to promote green remodeling. We have to get past the mentality of "newest" and "latest" and rediscover the value of "timeless" and "permanent." If you like your home, making it greener will give you all the more reason to love it as well as lower your bills.

Three Simple Plans for Greening Your Home

When I tell people I live in a green home, the first thing they ask me is, "Wow, so you have solar panels on the roof?"

Well, no, I don't. "What about one of those cool mini wind turbines in your yard?" Um, no, not that either. When I say instead that my house features the 3600 series Polysteel ICF wall system—one of the best building envelopes available for residential construction—I'm often met with a wandering gaze. What people don't realize is that the key to green building is an energy-efficient system. While renewable energy technologies can be effective accessories, they cannot offset the negative impact of a low-performing, inefficient structure. A tight building envelope is the most important feature to a green home.

This is one of the many challenges green builders face—in fact, one that sustainability professionals face in every industry. How do they show us that energy conservation matters most when we are programmed to believe that the solution to our dilemma lies within buying the latest gizmo? Informed green advocates know that conservation comes first.

Bryan Korba is the managing partner of Enpact Group, a sustainable real estate developer. His firm does everything from eco-sensitive design and architecture to green remodels. When I told Bryan I wanted to create a simple "Top 10" list of green remodeling tips by order of cost savings, he suggested I take a different tack. "Green remodeling is something people undertake for a number of reasons. Not all the reasons go back to cost savings. Some measures will save you money, others will improve your health, and still others promote a healthier planet."

Bryan's point encapsulates the message behind this book. It's similar to the idea of charity beginning at home or of putting your own oxygen mask on before helping the person next to you on the plane. If we begin with changes that directly improve our circumstances and shore up our resources, we'll have a greater supply to share with others as our vision expands.

The following plans provide a menu of options to help you make decisions based on your objectives. From numbers

1 to 25, these green tips can help you use less energy, reduce carbon emissions, lower your water usage, improve air quality, enhance your home's comfort, increase its value, and reduce your bills by as much as 50 percent. Go down the list and see what you can do now. To gain the full green advantage at home, plan to work in as many tips as possible within the next three years.

Plan #1: Save Money

Did you know the average home spends about $2,000 in energy each year? Many spend far more than that. "Energy cost inflation has increased dramatically over the past decade," says Craig Senglin, owner of Energy IQ. "At current rates, a US home owner in 2010 can expect their average monthly utility bills to exceed their mortgage payment within fifteen to twenty years! The era of cheap power has come to an end."

Do-It-Yourself Home Audit

Use the ENERGY STAR "Home Energy Yardstick" to compare your home's energy efficiency to similar homes across the country and get recommendations for energy-saving home improvements. If you don't have your bills, contact your utility for a twelve-month summary.

For more information, visit www.energystar.gov.

A green remodel beginning with your home's building envelope can significantly reduce your bills while increasing the value of your home.

Lee Hall, LEED consultant and project manager in the sustainable building industry, says the best place to begin a green remodel is through a procedure called "modeling." An energy auditor will use special tools, such as REM/Rate software, to prioritize energy efficiency upgrades in terms of impact and payback period. "Modeling enables you to see if those new windows that may cost $50,000 will bring their value back, or how long it will take you to pay for the radiant barrier in your attic," Lee says. "Our home is twelve years old. The energy audit cost us $500, which was deducted from the total when the work was completed." The energy auditors used a blower door test on Lee's home, which pressurizes the air to reveal leaks. "In my house," Lee says, "we discovered that the air-conditioning was being sucked into my attic through my sliding pocket doors as well as holes around fixtures. We had no idea." After plugging the holes and crevices with caulking, Lee was able to improve his home's air quality while lowering his bills.

Craig Senglin agrees. "I hear from a lot of clients who are initially very interested in installing a radiant barrier in their attic. They've heard all these advertisements promising amazing savings. But when I model their home in REM/Rate, we discover that adding $300 worth of solar screens on their windows will be five times more effective to lower their energy use than a $2,500 radiant barrier," he says. "Paying a small amount up front for this information will help you spend the least amount of money and ensure that your green remodel will pay off big in the long run."

Here are the top 25 priorities for a green remodel:

1. **Begin with a REM/Rate energy model of your home.** Hire an energy rater to do a HERS Index rating on your home prior to spending money on your remodel. This process enables the energy rater to simulate the impact of any and all upgrades to help you make logical decisions about where to make your investment. Making the suggested changes can save you 30 percent on your energy bills.

2. **Upgrade your HVAC or tune up your existing one.** You may have only six to ten high-demand days. Most of the time the air conditioner does not run at high demand. You can save money by replacing your air conditioner with a variable-speed model. If you're all electric, use heat pumps. Make sure these are serviced regularly.

3. **Install programmable thermostats.** Programmable thermostats have a very quick return on investment,

sometimes as fast as two months. These devices allow you to set the thermostat when you leave the house in order to achieve the desired temperature just before you walk through the door.

4. **Stop the bleeding!** Sealing and insulating your home's "envelope" is often the most cost-effective way to improve energy efficiency and comfort. A knowledgeable home owner or skilled contractor can save up to 20 percent on heating and cooling costs by sealing and insulating holes and crevices. For a free do-it-yourself guide to sealing and insulating, visit the Home Improvement section of www.energystar.gov.

5. **Replace all incandescent lightbulbs with compact fluorescent lightbulbs (CFLs).** In chapter 5, I suggested replacing five bulbs with CFLS. Now consider installing CFL bulbs throughout your entire house. CFLs use about 75 percent less energy and also produce 75 percent less heat than standard incandescent bulbs. Less energy and less heat mean the CFLs will save you about $30 or more in electricity costs over the life of each bulb.

6. **Get rid of can lights.** These are as bad as a chimney in terms of letting air escape. Also, they burn very hot and are prone to fire if there is insulation around them. If you cannot replace these, at least replace the bulbs with cool-burning fluorescents. To improve insulation, you can even go into the attic and put a Styrofoam cooler over each one.

7. **If you own a pool, get a new pool pump.** Swimming pool pumps are one of the top consumers of electricity in a home (following closely behind air-conditioning). If you can reduce the size of your swimming pool pump by even .25 horsepower, you should see a drop in your electric use. Select a variable speed pump that runs at a low speed. It will use 80 percent less energy and pay for itself in one year.

8. **Plug appliances into surge strips.** Devices such as Smart Strip and Wattstopper make it easy to minimize "vampire" energy loss, which occurs when microwave ovens, computers, TVs, digital appliances, electronic equipment, and associated chargers suck power even while turned off or in sleep or standby mode. Idle power from such appliances represents between 5 and 8 percent of a single family home's total electricity use per year. On average, that's the equivalent of one month's electricity bill. Priced anywhere from $30 to $90, surge strips can help you make a difference and save money with the flip of a switch.

9. **Add insulation to your attic.** To get the biggest savings, the easiest place to add insulation is usually in the attic. A quick way to see if you need more insulation is to look across your uncovered attic floor. If your insulation is level with or below the attic floor joists, you probably need to add more insulation. The recommended insulation level for most attics is R-38 (or about twelve to fifteen inches, depending on the insulation type). In the coldest climates, insulating up to R-49 is recommended.

10. **Upgrade to ENERGY STAR–qualified equipment.** Get rid of the old refrigerator in the garage. It's working against you! When buying an appliance, remember that it has two price tags: what you pay to take it home and what you pay for the energy and water it uses. ENERGY STAR–qualified appliances use 10 to 50 percent less energy and water than standard models. The money you save on your utility bills can more than make up for the cost of replacing inefficient washing machines, refrigerators, dishwashers, air conditioners, and dehumidifiers.

11. **Install a tankless water heater.** Tankless water heaters work on demand. When you turn on the hot water faucet, water flows past a gas burner or electric ele-

ment, heating it before it reaches the tap. This method uses less energy and wastes less water. The higher the energy factor (EF), the more efficient the heater. If you cannot replace your water heater, then wrap a blanket around your existing one to add insulation.

12. **Install an attic tent.** Typically, pull-down attic access stairs have a one-fourth-inch gap around the door. This gap is equivalent to a hole seven inches in diameter! An attic tent will stop the transfer of air and dirt between the attic and your living space.

13. **Replace your windows.** If you plan to replace windows in the near future or add new ones to a future home addition, use ENERGY STAR–qualified, low-emissive (low-e) windows. They could reduce your energy bill by as much as 15 percent. Look for a U-factor rating (which measures how well a product keeps heat from escaping) of 0.35 or less—the lower the better. In the South, the SHGC (solar heat gain coefficient) of windows is more important than the U-factor. SHGC measures the amount of solar radiation allowed through the glass. Generally, buildings in hot, sunny climates should employ window glass with SHGC of less than 0.50. A typical-size home with these windows can save up to $100 per year when compared to homes with clear, double-paned windows, or up to four times that amount when compared to single-pane windows. Modeling will help you determine the kind of return you can get on windows.

Plan #2: Save Your Health

Let's consider the evidence. Women who work from home are at a 54 percent higher risk of cancer. Since 1982 breast cancer has increased by 26 percent, becoming the number one killer of women between the ages of 35 and 54. Since 1980 asthma has increased by 600 percent. Is there any common link between these seemingly disparate studies? Scientists are linking these increases at least in part to harmful pollutants in our air. While indoor pollutants stem from a number of sources, there is a lot you can do to your home to reduce exposure to pollutants such as dust, smoke, mold, fungi, and VOCs (volatile organic compounds).

14. **Test for fresh air.** Now that you've sealed your house and your ducts, it is a good idea to measure the amount of fresh air you're receiving. Point #1 above was to perform a HERS rating or index on your home. Now do it again! A home should have approximately .35 air changes per hour, though that depends on many factors. Most remodeled homes will not be greater than that, but if yours is, then consider some type of ventilation system. Exhaust, supply, or balanced ventilation techniques are available. Energy Recovery Ventilators (ERVs) are excellent whole-house ventilating systems that also transfer heat, cool air, and humidification between the exhausted air and the new air.

15. **Use low- or non-VOC paints.** Paint is a contributing factor to poor indoor air quality and can emit harmful chemicals such as VOCs for years (although the majority of those emissions dissipates within several weeks of application). The best nontoxic paints are Zero VOC paints, but they cost around $30 per gallon. For a low-cost alternative, try low-VOC paints.

16. **Replace carpet with greener flooring when possible.** Carpet can be loaded with VOCs. If you have a concrete foundation like we do, you can finish it for a clean, stylish, and virtually maintenance-free effect. Our concrete floors are etched with an acid stain, which reacts with the concrete to give it color, and topped with a paste wax finish. The ambient temperature of the ground is 60 degrees year-round, so our floors stay cool in the summer and moderate in the winter. We use accent rugs

to create a warmer feel. If concrete doesn't work for you, consider other sustainable options such as bamboo or reclaimed wood. If you must have carpet, ask for carpets with the "Green Label Plus" certification. This initiative certifies that carpets have passed independent laboratory tests for emissions from thirteen notorious chemicals.

17. **Use water filters.** A good water filter can remove 99 percent of the impurities in water. It can also save a lot of money and waste from buying bottled water.

Plan #3: Save the Planet

The residential sector is responsible for approximately 22 percent of carbon emissions in the United States. Reducing these carbon emissions and improving air quality are deep green concerns. The EPA reports that by 2013, an estimated 36 states will experience water shortages as a result of increased water usage and inefficient water management from aging regional infrastructures. Also, although water is presently the "redheaded stepchild" of the program, it will become the leading concern in many cities as this precious resource becomes more expensive.

18. **Harvest rainwater.** My neighbor Carey has lived in his home for twenty years. After taking most of the measures in the above two sections, he's now working on Plan #3. Carey invited me over to see the rainwater capture system in his backyard. "The technology is still new, so it takes a little creativity to figure out how best to use it in your yard," he said. Carey rigged a system linking eight sixty-gallon barrels together on a platform to accommodate spillage. The barrels fill up completely after two days of regular rain. A whole system can cost around $200, but even one barrel lets you take advantage of free water for your garden without taking up too

much space. Cities such as San Francisco and Austin are even hosting how-to workshops and offering rebates on rainwater catchment tanks.

19. **Install water-saving showerheads.** Look for a low-flow showerhead that uses 2.5 gallons a minute or less. These inexpensive, easy-to-install showerheads can reduce water use by 50 percent and still provide an invigorating shower. In addition to reducing your water bill, you'll save energy costs for your water heater.

20. **Use dual-flush toilets.** The typical toilet uses 1.5 gallons of water per flush. Dual-flush toilets handle solid and liquid waste differently, giving the user a choice of flushes that help to conserve water. You can conserve on your own by flushing less regularly.

21. **Recycle gray water.** Any water that has been used in the home, except water from toilets, is called *gray water*. Dish, shower, sink, and laundry water comprise 50 to 80 percent of residential waste water. This may be re-used for other purposes, especially landscape irrigation. Most cities still don't permit gray-water usage, but technologies are changing all the time, so this could change sooner than we think.

22. **Use a renewable energy provider.** Solar, wind-power, and geothermal applications are undergoing rapid transformation. I consider these "advanced green" for home installation, but most of us have access to cleaner electricity through our utility company. Mike and I have been using 100 percent renewable energy from Green Mountain Energy for ten years. Knowing we are contributing to cleaner air helps take the sting out of paying energy bills.

23. **Go solar.** Installing solar panels requires an investment, but tax incentives can cut costs by two-thirds, and once you've paid for the system, your power is free. Solar shingles are another exciting way to harness the sun's power on your roof. If your state does not yet offer tax

incentives to reduce the expense of solar installations to a manageable amount, try opting for smaller applications such as a solar-powered gate.

24. **Plant trees.** Give your home some natural shade with abundant trees. Your kids will love to help you plant them and watch them grow over the years. Not only can you save $150 or more in annual energy costs, but you'll also leave a legacy. We joined the Arbor Day Foundation for $15 and received 10 free trees! Visit www.arborday.org to learn more.

25. **Green your decor.** Consignment stores, outdoor bazaars, local art shows, antique shops, and websites such as www.craigslist.org and www.freecycle.org offer quality furniture and accessories you won't be able to find in stores. Buy secondhand items at a fraction of the cost while preserving the planet from excess carbon emissions created in manufacturing and transportation. Buying antique furniture is also a form of using reclaimed wood while getting the added benefits of uniqueness and patina. I bought a French solid oak secretary desk on Craig's List for $150. After spending another $150 on antique black paint and new hardware, the piece resembles ones I've seen for over $1,000 in stores. You can also support local artists. I bought two oil paintings done by local artisans for $15 apiece. I had them framed at a local shop, and now they hang in my living room. They are beautiful, original, and green.

Life Imitates Art: From Green Remodeling to Green Living

Shortly after 9-11 Ashleigh Bull was in the midst of planning a home addition when she had an epiphany. What if she could use this as an opportunity to make the world a better place? "When the Towers fell, it was like a switch went on," Ashleigh says. "I wanted to do something but didn't know where to start. This project was right in front of me, so I started with our home."

I first met Ashleigh's husband Jon during a client project for his law firm, Gardere Wynne Sewell LLP. An attorney and a member of the firm's "green team," Jon advocates for greener practices in the legal industry. He took the initiative to devise a special system for having lengthy documents sent to the copier for double-sided printing and then loaded into double-ringed binders for easy reading. Remembering Jon's knack for coming up with inventive ways to be greener, I asked him for a tour of his green remodel.

The Bulls live in Lakewood, a Dallas neighborhood boasting mature trees, updated ranch houses, genteel Tudors, and a number of historically significant properties. The Bulls incorporated sensible green features into a striking Southwest-inspired decor and managed to increase the size of their

Green Home and Living Resource Center

GreenHomeGuide.com is a coast-to-coast online network of green building, remodeling, and decorating professionals. Sponsored by the US Green Building Council, the site allows anyone to "Ask a Pro" for advice on bathrooms, bedrooms, countertops, energy efficiency, flooring, furniture, kitchens, landscaping, nursery, paint and coatings, and stone and tile.

Other websites are loaded with up-to-date product reviews. Here are a few:
www.greenamerica.com
www.sustainlane.com
www.treehugger.com

home while lowering their carbon footprint. Walking us around the house, Ashleigh said, "We added on 1,200 square feet, increasing our home to a total of 3,000 square feet. At the same time, we lowered our bills by 30 percent." The Bulls attribute the savings to a 19 SEER HVAC system, a tankless water heater, double-paned windows, compact fluorescent lighting, and enhanced attic insulation—in the form of recycled blue jeans.

Walking through the house, we stopped in the kitchen so I could admire the counters, which are made of locally harvested mesquite wood and polished with a nut-oil stain. An oversized ceramic sink, oil-rubbed fixtures, and a cast-iron waffle pan give the room a vintage feel. By commingling traditional design elements with innovative, repurposed accessories such as kitchen stools made from old bicycle parts, the Bulls have created a stylish, upbeat, and comfortable effect. You might call it "green chic."

Walking me outside, the Bulls showed how they did away with the garage to make room for a larger garden. "We started this garden four years ago. It's been such a learning process. It's neat to see the plants begin to seed themselves and grow naturally on their own." Next to the garden are Ashleigh's compost pile and a clothesline. Parked in the driveway is a Prius. Hmmm . . . all the symbols of a granola-variety environmentalist, but you'd never know it by looking at Ashleigh and Jon. Ashleigh, a petite blonde who works part-time as the school nurse at her children's elementary school, doesn't exactly scream "eco-activist." I asked her what it is that motivates her to so thoroughly weave green into her lifestyle. "This is a family project," she says. "We are teaching our kids about environmental stewardship by incorporating eco-friendly ways into our home life."

The Bulls' brand of green enhances their home's warmth and appeal. For such an emphasis on practicality, Ashleigh has hit all the high notes on the design front too. Walking back into the house, I take in the vivid colors, original artwork, and stylish Arts & Crafts furnishings. Walls are painted periwinkle, gold, and blue with EnviroSafe low-VOC paint. Daughter Rosalie has a hand-painted (water-based) ponderosa pine bed, a piece of whimsical furniture produced by a local artisan using earth-friendly practices.

"Piece by piece we have accumulated furniture and possessions that have been responsibly manufactured," Ashleigh said. "It's a great look and a wonderful feeling." Jon added, "We're staying home more now." He pointed to the kitchen. "We cook more as a family. We make bread, waffles, homemade pizza, and anything we can with herbs from our garden. It feels like we have everything we need right here."

Considering the savings, health benefits, and intangible payoffs such as comfort, peace of mind, and family harmony, a green remodel is the ideal starting point for making a difference. Once you build your green foundation, you may find yourself looking around for ways to extend sustainability into your lifestyle as the Bull family did. Chapters 10 and 11 offer fun and easy tips to help you make the most of greener living.

10

Urban Oasis or
Sustainable Suburb?

The American city should be a collection
of communities where every member has a
right to belong. It should be a place where
every man feels safe on his streets and in the
house of his friends. It should be a place
where each individual's dignity and self-
respect is strengthened by the respect and
affection of his neighbors.

Lyndon B. Johnson,
36th president of the United States

Have you read Laura Ingalls Wilder? If not, you've probably seen *Little House on the Prairie*, the TV series
chronicling Laura's growing-up years in a family of pioneers
in the Midwestern frontier in the late 1800s. Mike and his
brother used to call it *Little Disaster on the Prairie* because
the plot consistently featured emotional scenes of someone
dying, going blind, going away, or going broke. Most episodes

did bring me to tears, but not always tears of sadness. Call me sentimental, but who wouldn't weep over Laura taking an after-school job as a seamstress to buy Ma a new oven, or Pa working himself sick to hold on to the farm?

When Laura Ingalls Wilder started writing her classic series in 1932, she didn't know it would make her famous. Upon completion of eight volumes in 1943, she had painted a lasting literary portrait of pioneer life. She also achieved the American Dream—twice, in fact, as the dream itself is something of a moving target.

The original version of the American Dream began with the Declaration of Independence. It evolved as the pioneers pursued their rights to life, liberty, and happiness by settling the country, sowing the land, putting down roots, having families, and building towns. By the time Wilder's works were published, the dream had begun to morph into the pursuit of success and stardom, or, at a minimum, a big house in the suburbs with two cars and plenty of toys. For the next fifty years, we pursued the dream through a cycle of work and spending that, at some point, moved past progress into excess. By the beginning of the twenty-first century, the dream turned to a nightmare as families across America lost their McMansions to foreclosure and their portfolios to a devastated economy.

> *I am beginning to learn that it is the sweet, simple things of life which are the real ones after all.*
>
> Laura Ingalls Wilder, American author and pioneer

Many are in the sudden position of starting over. Soured by debt and bankruptcy, some are growing nostalgic for the old-fashioned family farm. A number of people are taking creative steps to revive the agrarian tradition in fresh forms suitable to urban and suburban lifestyles. While some are doing so out of necessity, others are striving for stronger social bonds or spiritual renewal through greater interaction with nature—and each other. For those of us caught somewhere in between, we are fortunate to have examples of twenty-first-century pioneers who've gotten a head start in carving out sustainable communities for themselves. You may not think you need a chicken coop, a solar cooker, or a community garden, but cultivating these hobbies gives you a good excuse to hang out with your neighbors, teach your kids the value of the earth's resources, and save some money too.

Tales of a Chicken Mentor

Julie Dreher lives in historic Junius Heights, a nearby neighborhood of 1920s bungalows in varying states of restoration. I first read about her in the book *Crunchy Cons*, her husband Rod's highly readable treatise on the "conservative counterculture," a phenomenon that is quietly reshaping American politics. Rod is brilliant at turning simple observations into artful descriptions that make homeschooling and raising chickens seem like ideas one might actually want to try.

After meeting Rod during an environmental panel discussion, he suggested I speak to his wife about my book. Wondering if their real lives would be like the fairy tale I perceived in *Crunchy Cons*, I readily accepted the invitation. Preparing for the visit, I wasn't sure who intimidated me more: Rod the intellectual or Julie the superwoman. I knew that Julie, who has her MBA, now homeschools her three children while cooking meals from scratch and juggling a multitude of agrarian experiments. Any one of these activities might send me into a tailspin, almost certainly resulting in Mike getting his head bitten off as soon as he walks through the door. But as I judged from Rod's writing, Julie manages her parental responsibilities with grace while cultivating a cozy retreat for her husband after a hard day's work.

After spending three delightful hours with the Drehers, I was gratified to see how their simple mode of living brings joy to their family. Their home is just as Rod described. "The beauty of the little wooden house is its elegant simplicity," he writes. "This is a house with dignity and humanity. It starts from the sidewalk, looking at the façade, at the low-pitched roof, the wide-eyed eaves, the brick chimney, and the square-columned porch."[1] It is from this porch that Rod first welcomed me. He walked me through the sun-filled living room, past the ample fireplace, and into a dining room lined with books and a long wooden table. Julie walked in, smiling, and greeted me warmly. Moving through their cozy kitchen and onto the back porch, we ended the tour in their back-yard garden. Rod handed me a cup of hot coffee and invited me to sit in a wooden recliner with a footstool. Relaxing in the warm sun, I enjoyed the breeze while looking over the spacious backyard replete with vegetable gardens and three merry children chasing chickens. I could see the charm. The Drehers have truly created an urban oasis.

"I had a very suburban upbringing," Julie said. "I still have friends here who I'm close to, but I'm not sure they get why I'm doing this." It is curious, in fact, how she got from point A to point Z, but that is precisely why I wanted to meet her. So many of us see the finished product, but we never understand the transformation process. "When we were living in New York, I loved our home in Brooklyn," Julie said. "We would walk to locally owned stores to do our shopping. We knew all the people we bought from. We had our favorite restaurants. Moving back to Dallas, I wanted to retain that connection to my community. I'm glad I've found that we can lead a similar lifestyle here too. We began by shopping at the farmer's market for our produce, although now we grow a lot of it ourselves.

"Homeschooling happened for us in the same way," Julie continued. "I did it in New York because I thought I could give my kids a better education than the public schools could. When we moved here, I set out to find other families in the area that were homeschooling. It has been a great way to build a community." I asked Julie if she thought everyone is cut out for homeschooling. "When I first came up with the idea in New York, I thought I was prepared, that I knew everything there was to know. But then I actually had children," Julie said with a laugh. "Since then, I've had to play with this a number of ways to see how it can work. There is no one-size-fits-all approach. The best advice I could give is for us to realize that, as moms, we're learning all the time. When it comes to homeschooling, it really doesn't matter what educational background you have so much as your circumstances and your desire to take this on."

For Julie, it has been rewarding but also humbling. After Rod published his book about the virtues of homeschooling, they had to turn around and send one child to school for several years. "Matthew started reading at age two and a half. He was academically advanced but socially behind. He's doing much better now, so he's back at home. From that experience I've learned to take things year by year," Julie said.

Julie's making a lot of sense. I can relate to wanting to escape the burden of materialism in order to imbue my family with more meaningful values. And I'm all for promoting a love of nature, but how does raising chickens fit into this ethos? "It just seemed like the next logical step. I've been trying to reduce our environmental impact by recycling and composting, but you can't compost everything. By introducing chickens into the equation, we keep food waste to a minimum. Not only that, we get about five eggs a day. It's more of a closed system," Julie said. "Besides, the kids love them."

Homeschooling

Julie recommends K[12], a national organization that provides any child access to an exceptional curriculum and tools to maximize success in life, regardless of geographic, financial, or demographic circumstances. K[12] is a leader in providing individualized, one-to-one learning solutions to students from kindergarten through high school across the country.

For more information, visit www.k12.com.

Looking at it ecologically, it makes perfect sense. I looked across the yard and saw Lucas holding a chick as cute as a bunny. "I've got a friend who decided to do the same thing. She calls me her chicken mentor." We walked over to the chicken coop, and she handed me an egg. "Here, take this home with you. You'll notice that the yolk is almost orange. Fresh eggs are the best."

Then and there, I put "chicken coop" on my wish list. I asked her what advice she has for others thinking about going this direction. "Don't think this happens overnight. I have tried a lot of things that haven't worked," she said, pointing out a few tired-looking potted plants to illustrate her point. "But the important thing is to try."

Rod invited me into the house for a bowl of white bean and squash soup, served with broccoli and a salad Julie prepared from her garden. It was one of the tastiest vegetarian meals I've ever eaten. Rod served sparkling water mixed with pomegranate juice, and we continued our discussion.

"Urban Chicken" Underground

An underground urban chicken movement is sweeping across the United States. Cities such as Ann Arbor, Michigan; Ft. Collins, Colorado; and South Portland, Maine, have all recently voted to allow residents to raise backyard poultry. Keeping your own chickens is a great way to enjoy fresh eggs for less money. A quick online search brings up loads of free instructions for building your own coop as well as opportunities for you to buy a ready-made coop for as low as $300.

For the Drehers, nothing is mundane. Everything has meaning. They call it "sacramental living," something akin to but deeper than sustainable living. The Drehers, who each grew up in Protestant families, ultimately found a more fulfilling worship experience in the Orthodox Christian church. Drawing on this deep-seated spiritual ethic and their Southern roots, the Drehers intentionally orient their lives around home and hearth. It's hard to believe when I first read about their lifestyle; I suspected they couldn't really like it as much as they said. But as I sat with their family at the table, their contentment was contagious. One gets the sense that in this house, it is okay—in fact, preferable—to be imperfect. Behind the curtain are two very approachable people muddling through the challenges of parenthood and home ownership like the rest of us, but with a level of peace that goes beyond the pale.

Julie and I continued talking after Rod left for an appointment. "I love Craig's List," Julie said. "I've met this whole little community of people who share stuff with each other. You can learn a lot about your neighbors this way. Some leave thank-you notes, some want to meet me, others just want to drop something by the curb. Some people are always willing to take old things off people's hands. Others are always giving things away." Looking around, I noticed a hand-carved cuckoo clock hanging on the wall. On the table rested a cast-iron ceremonial teapot intricately decorated with an Asian motif. Like everything else in the house, these possessions radiated authenticity, unlike the usual bric-a-brac from Tuesday Morning. "These were gifts that people gave to Rod. The kids adore the clock. It plays Edelweiss. We had another one, but we gave it to another family when we got this one."

Gracious and convivial hosts, the Drehers have discovered that the secret to living well is to give away more than you receive. As far as I can tell, that is also the secret to building a community. Altogether, the experience made me want to go home, pull a few books off the shelves, untidy the living room, stir up a pitcher of iced tea, and invite the neighbors over to put their feet up on my coffee table.

The Comeback of Solar Cooking

I knew my neighbor Carey had culinary talent because he's made us everything from German chocolate cake to seasoned grilled lamb. Last week he surprised me with a huge helping of his latest dish: homemade herbed chicken and rice with fresh-baked bread—straight out of his solar cooker.

I was intrigued by this food connoisseur's interest in preparing his favorite recipes in a solar-powered oven. What does this crazy contraption look like? How does it operate? Dying to know more, I wrangled a dinner invitation to Carey's house to see his oven in action and to taste more of his glorious solar cooking. When I arrived, Carey walked me outside to his back patio. "Here it is," he said, gesturing to a cube-like structure with mirrored sides that flop open, spanning roughly two feet by two feet. Inside the mirrored compartment rests a black pot. "This oven heats up to over 300 degrees, and I've seen it go up as high as 450," Carey said. "I use Granite Ware pots inside because the black surface absorbs the heat." Carey opened the lid to show me the bubbling stew.

Inside we kept talking over a delightful dinner of garden-fresh salad and solar-baked specialties that included sourdough bread and beef tagine flavored with Porcini mushrooms and mozzarella cheese. I asked Carey what gave him the inclination to take on solar cooking. "Well, after taking all these steps to put insulation in my house and install radiant barrier," he said, "I began to wonder why I was letting my hot oven counteract all the work that my air conditioner was doing to ward off the summer heat." I nodded in agreement. But why use the solar oven on this chilly March evening? "Well," Carey explained, "once I discovered how well it worked last August, I decided to use it year-round."

Carey has two ovens. The Global Sun Oven, the more flexible of the two, has a convenient carrying case, can be operated by a child, and retails for around $289. The HotPot, made by Solar Household Energy, operates more like a true crock-pot. It slow-cooks between 200 and 225 degrees, which is perfectly adequate but takes more time. The HotPot models range from $79 to $99.

Solar cooking may remain a novelty in America, but then again, it may not. World Bank now estimates that around two billion people suffer from energy poverty. We could be one or two natural disasters away from needing easy access to solar cooking ourselves. John and Robin Robertson are getting a head start on heading off disaster with their book *Apocalypse Chow: How to Eat Well When the Power Goes Out.*

The Solar Cooker Project

The Solar Cooker Project, a wonderful mission sponsored by Jewish World Watch, helps refugee women in Darfur. The Solar Cooker Project protects women from being raped while they collect firewood and also provides them with income opportunities. They can make money through manufacturing solar cookers, training others to use the cookers, and making carrying bags to increase the cookers' life span.

For more information, visit www.jewishworldwatch.org.

Alarmism aside, solar cooking is a good idea for Westerners, but it's essential for quality of life in the developing world. This makes solar cookers the ideal mission opportunity for groups or individuals. One meal at a time, Carey is reducing carbon emissions, saving precious natural resources, reducing deforestation, supporting the growth of a clean technology industry (he also drives a Prius), and advocating for greener living. In fact, Carey extended his mission abroad by sending a solar cooker to his friends in Chile. But he doesn't regard these decisions as mission work, just good ideas. "I'm not trying to make a statement or anything," he said. "I just thought my friends in South America could use one. Energy costs are skyrocketing down there."

I'm humbled by the simple acts I see neighbors perform every day to do their part—reminding me over and over that there is so much more to environmental stewardship than just talking about it.

Cultivating an Urban Oasis

Some of my neighbors here in Little Forest Hills, a neighborhood made famous by the documentary "Subdivided," will have a field day with me for writing a book about being green. All things being relative, my trek toward sustainable living may make me "radical" or "leftist" in certain circles, but here in this neighborhood, I'm considered pretty conventional.

An offbeat nook of smaller-scale homes amid an urban forest, Little Forest Hills residents are an eclectic mix of photographers, entrepreneurs, and artists, with some professionals and a few aging hippies thrown in. A hodgepodge of ages, political affiliations, and socioeconomic backgrounds, the residents have a motto described by the signs in their yards: "Keep Little Forest Hills Funky." Buffered by neighborhoods with homes priced in the range of $500,000 to $1.4 million, most homes in this neighborhood are valued at a fraction of the bottom figure. The price and location across the street from White Rock Lake make it attractive to younger families, people who work downtown, outdoor enthusiasts, retirees, and people who want to escape the monotony of a typical subdivision.

When my husband and I got started on our building project, we didn't know it would cause a stir among neighborhood veterans who thought it should remain an artists' community. One man even said, "This is not a neighborhood for rich professionals." Others who had also been here for decades were thrilled to see families like ours investing in the neighborhood.

The fight for Little Forest Hills is indicative of similar ones erupting in neighborhoods across America. I can understand both sides. On the one hand, residents in smaller, older homes don't want to be outpriced by newer, bigger homes and higher property taxes. On the other hand, outdated or neglected houses that can't fetch a good price on the market end up turning into rentals. This doesn't secure safety, stability, or the quality of a neighborhood's infrastructure. Neighborhoods that don't retain development in line with demand will not sustain property values, and most people's largest asset is their home.

Ironically, political strife ended up bringing some of our community closer together as we found ourselves teaming up to go on the defensive. We spent three months going to weekly meetings and knocking on neighbors' doors, asking them to sign our petitions. The whole mess ended up going before the city council, which ultimately voted against the restrictions brought forth by the other side. We're now well into a healing process that is restoring a sense of community.

While urban living is the more sustainable choice, situations like the one I described represent the trade-offs to choosing the urban over the suburban experience. Urban neighborhoods require you to get comfortable with different social, economic, and ethnic backgrounds. Schools are another issue, sometimes requiring urban families to use private schools or to homeschool. Apart from these hurdles, the benefits are numerous. Mike's downtown commute is less than twenty minutes. The park is a block and a half away, which has turned into a lovely meeting place for families each evening before dinner. The neighborhood association, which hosts the annual Fourth of July parade, organizes committees for everything from animal rescue to wine tasting. The kids on our street play at each other's houses and attend each other's birthday parties.

What has been very exciting for me is to see how neighbors share my enthusiasm for sustainability. Kimberly and Angela next door are adding their kitchen scraps to my compost. My neighbor Amy gave me an eco-friendly "G" diaper, which helped me save a few disposable diapers from going into a landfill. (She also makes the best cookies I've ever tasted.) Alan, the green home builder, and his wife Pam host several parties a year where they bring young and old together.

On top of this, we've joined the community church (a six-minute walk from home), and we enrolled our daughter in St. Bernard, the school next door to the church. By supporting the associations directly in our community, we now have several hundred more people in the immediate area who can help us look out for our kids, protect our property, discourage crime, and increase our network.

Has it been perfect all the time? No, but nothing is. I will say that so far we've found more of what we're looking for here than anywhere else. The whole setup reminds me of the way the townspeople on *Little House on the Prairie* used the beloved one-room schoolhouse for school, church, and town hall meetings. Laura Ingalls Wilder lived in a real community. This childhood memory stuck so thoroughly that I'm beginning to think I subconsciously set out to create a "little house in the city." If you have a pioneering spirit, you can make a home out of any frontier, even an urban one.

Not Your Typical Subdivision

"The American suburb as we know it is dying," Bryan Walsh said in his article in *Time*. The title, "Recycling the Suburbs," is idea #2 on the magazine's list of "10 Ideas That Are Changing the World." The article points out that in 2008, an estimated 148,000 retail and big-box stores closed, but this isn't the only indicator of declining values in properties outside the urban core. Other factors include a steady decline in the percentage of households with kids, and a growing preference for urban amenities. The Metropolitan Institute at Virginia Tech predicts that by 2025 there will be a surplus of 22 million large-lot homes (on one-sixth of an acre or more) in the United States. "The suburban dream of the big house and the big lawn is vanishing."[2]

I'm not so sure about that last part. Admittedly, I used to think that outside-the-loop living looked dreadful. Cookie-cutter subdivisions, concrete parking lots, and conformity at every turn. But my hard line is beginning to soften. As much as I love our home, there are moments, such as when I'm paying for property taxes or private school tuition, when I dismiss my beef with the burbs long enough to think, *What if?* Looking past the fast-food joints and strip malls, I see a haven of safe schools, cozy communities, convenient shopping, activities for kids, open spaces, and friendly faces. I'd be lying if I said I couldn't see the attraction.

One worry interrupts my pastoral reverie as I ponder modern-day Mayberry. I cannot seem to reconcile sustainability with suburbia. Does a green suburb even exist? Thus began my quest for signs of green life beyond the city limits.

I didn't have to travel very far. Montgomery Farm, located about thirty miles north of Dallas, is a community founded on the ideal that open meadows, woodland habitat, and native wildlife can be conserved and enhanced through inspired planning and design. Situated on five hundred acres of pristine prairie and forest in Collin County, Montgomery Farm is a nonpolluting, energy-efficient, sustainable development adjacent to a nature conservancy.

Sharing a picnic lunch with developer and owner Philip Williams, I found myself looking out over the same unspoiled vista seen by pioneers more than a century ago. "Before European man showed up," Philip said, "most of the land was forested with blackland prairies. The land was first cleared around the time of the Civil War to be used for cotton farming. My grandfather bought it and rehabilitated it." The tree outside the window of the old farmhouse that serves as Philip's office is the second-largest cedar elm in the world, a testament to the dedication of the family to preserve the past.

Apart from the obvious preservation of open natural spaces, which most developers would have replaced with a golf course or swimming complex, I wondered what specifically makes this a sustainable community. "My grandfather was a horse farmer and a conservationist," Philip said. "When he set out to revitalize the land, covering up the terraces left from cotton farming with gently rolling hills and native grasses, he did so with the intent to create a self-contained ecological system. When he left the land to my mother, she formed a nature conservancy out of it. Montgomery Farm as a residential and commercial development is the fourth iteration of this land, but we're still adhering to the original conservation principles my grandfather valued."

Philip focuses on environmental sustainability through energy-efficient housing and water conservation. Montgomery Farm does not engage in developing the land at breakneck speed. Instead, development is based on present demand for quality structures with thoughtful attention to the preservation of open space.

"It's the role of a good developer to treat public space as public art. Good aesthetics lends identity to a place," Philip says. Montgomery Farm hired an internationally recognized artist to develop an artful sculpture of a windmill and a large working cistern. "We've created functional art that draws in the eye and ignites the imagination, even for those who don't understand the deeper meaning. These artistic elements simply make the drive down our streets—that is, a slice of everyday life—more enjoyable."

Lee Hall, who heads up the sustainable development arm of Philip's company, Emerson Partners, shares wisdom he applied to the Montgomery Farm project. "Sustainability is about making a place that a human being wants to be in. Good sustainability has the natural aspect, but at a minimum, it's all about the individual. It's about good architecture and quality. Once you build something, it needs to stand the test of time." Lee explains that from a developmental standpoint, we need to learn to design around health, not just the automobile. "City codes need to be reviewed and either trashed or amended so city services can get away from codes solely related to driving," Lee says. "For example, when we were building one area of Montgomery Farm, we had to work with the City of Allen to reinterpret the city code to allow for more narrow streets. The city codes have been through so many iterations that in some ways they have been rendered arbitrary."

Developers who want to fully execute their vision must be willing to collaborate closely with the municipal government. According to Lee, the key to making suburbia more sustainable is to "educate, educate, educate. Green is not about the gizmo. It's a building and development science that demands systems thinking."

The New Urbanism: What to Look For in a Community

Greener urban development is an extension of the New Urbanism movement that began in the late 1970s as a reaction to suburban sprawl. The heart of New Urbanism is in the design of the neighborhoods. According to Andres Duany, town planner, architect, and founder of the Congress for the New Urbanism, an authentic neighborhood contains key elements that can be designed into existing neighborhoods and planned developments.

For more information, visit www.cnu.org/intro_to_new_urbanism.

Although there are barriers to true sustainable design in the suburbs, there is much progress to celebrate. Kipp Nash, for example, is a part-time bus driver who formed an organization called Community Roots. With help from his neighbors and other volunteers, Nash is providing locally grown organic food by creating a working organic farm on the front lawns of the Martin Acres subdivision in Boulder, Colorado.

Nash, a former apprentice at an organic farm, came up with the idea of using the yards of willing volunteers to create a microfarm that can feed fifty families. He took out an ad in the neighborhood newsletter asking for space for a garden. "The whole project snowballed when we planted in our next-door neighbors' front yard," he says. "Then everyone got curious." The end result was the Community Roots CSA (community-supported agriculture) program, in which families and individuals pay in advance for a share of the weekly harvest. Although he's proud of the organic vegetables he puts on people's tables, Nash is proudest of how the program connects people. "It's awesome watching neighbors meet each other as they gather at the CSA pickup stand for their share of the week's crops," he says. "That alone makes all the work worthwhile."[3]

11

Green Games Your Kids Will Love

> Given a chance, a child will bring the con-
> fusion of the world to the woods, wash it
> in the creek, turn it over to see what lives
> on the unseen side of that confusion. . . .
> In nature, a child finds freedom, fantasy,
> and privacy: a place distant from the adult
> world, a separate peace.
>
> Richard Louv,
> author of *Last Child in the Woods*

For me, this is the final chapter in my green journey, but for others it could be the most logical and fulfilling place to begin. Now that I'm fully practicing at home what I preach to companies, I finally understand why sustainability is such a difficult concept for people to grasp. How removed have we been from the sheer process of nature, of food growing, of waste decomposing into earth? Getting ecology on paper is one thing, but getting our hands dirty is another. There is nothing like tending your own garden to put your family in touch with what we are trying so hard to protect.

The ideas in this brief chapter could easily fall under a different heading, but I prefer to view them as games. Like

Mary Poppins says, "In every job that must be done, there is an element of fun. When you find the fun, it becomes a game!" (Okay, my family has a slight addiction to Walt Disney movies—we're still working on that.) Here's a spoonful of sugar to help the medicine go down: *you don't have to be an expert.* For most urban and suburban dwellers, the idea of tending a garden, composting, or bird watching is novel, if not altogether intimidating. Forget about becoming a master gardener or ornithologist. Just get your kids outside and have fun with it!

> *Man must feel the earth to know himself and recognize his values. . . . God made life simple. It is man who complicates it.*
>
> Charles A. Lindbergh,
> American aviator, author,
> inventor, and explorer

I've also included some ideas for indoor enthusiasts. Rain or shine, there are loads of projects you can undertake with your family to bring a little more nature into your world.

Organic Gardening for Beginners

Tending a garden must be instinctive to humans. There is no other way to explain why I am embracing it with such enthusiasm. To say I am not the outdoorsy type is an understatement. I dislike dirt and have an almost pathological fear of bugs (except spiders, only because they remind me of *Charlotte's Web*). How many of us wouldn't prefer sitting inside the air-conditioning or a screened porch to digging around in the dirt while getting chewed up by chiggers? And yet, I have an irrepressible urge to do so anyway.

I began with containers and just recently graduated to a small plot in my backyard. Now I delight in seeing pots of colorful spring annuals outside my door. I regularly use herbs from my garden of mint, parsley, lavender, oregano, and rosemary. I make fresh pesto from my basil plants, which grow large enough for the neighbors to enjoy too. Spring 2009 marked my first season of growing tomatoes, peppers, and cucumbers. As this book goes to print, I'm planting my first garden with lettuce, collards, cauliflower, and dill.

I started this as a fun hobby, but someday it could become a necessity. Did you know that during World Wars I and II, the US government asked its citizens to plant gardens in order to support the war effort? In 1943 Americans planted over twenty million "Victory Gardens," and the harvest accounted for nearly a third of all the vegetables consumed in the country that year. One of these Victory Gardens was planted on the White House lawn by Eleanor Roosevelt. In March 2009, First Lady Michelle Obama brought vegetable gardening back in vogue when she broke ground on her own White House garden. "I wanted to be able to bring what I learned to a broader base of people," Mrs. Obama said. "And what better way to do it than to plant a vegetable garden in the South Lawn of the White House?"[1] If she can demonstrate leadership by planting a garden on her lawn, so can any one of us.

You just never know in these rapidly changing times what will happen. Gardening as a family or as a community effort is not drudgery but a productive pastime. You can find instructions all over the internet to help you get started. Here are my favorite resources:

A real delicious heirloom tomato is one of the sweetest things that you'll ever eat. My children know the difference, and that's how I've been able to get them to try different things.

First Lady Michelle Obama

- **DirtDoctor.com** is run by Howard Garrett, a national radio show host and the author of more than fourteen books on organic gardening. You can listen to his podcasts and gain access to a number of free resources on his site.

- **GardenGuides.com** offers how-to advice for container gardening, family crafts, installing a lily pond, and pretty much anything else related to gardening. The website includes networking functionality to help you find answers to your gardening questions.
- **OrganicGardeningGuru.com** contains loads of step-by-step articles, favorite resources, and everything you need to know to become an organic gardener.

Easy-Does-It Composting

Now that I've taken the step of planting my first vegetable garden, I'm ready to learn some of the lessons I willfully ignored during high school biology. Fortunately I found out that you don't have to know how to dissect worms to properly care for a garden.

I was chatting over coffee with my friend Pat Gibbons, who owns the online store Green Earth Market. "I really do want to compost because ecologically it feels like the right thing to do," I confided to Pat, "but I can't bear worms." Reassuringly, Pat said, "Well, there are ways around that. My store has some products that can help you get started." We jumped online, and he showed me different composting options. I asked, "Which products do you recommend to set up a system that can help me get food scraps from my kitchen to my backyard on a consistent basis?" He recommended the Tumbleweed Tumbler Composter and the Composting Accessory Kit, which can hold the scraps in my kitchen using 100 percent biodegradable bags until I'm ready to add them to the tumbler outside.

> *You will find something far greater in the woods than you will find in books. Stones and trees will teach you that which you will never learn from masters.*
>
> St. Bernard of Clairvaux, French Cistercian monk

I'm loving my new kitchen compost kit and tumbler. My daughter Jordan is running around the yard picking up leaves and putting them in it. When we have leftover salad, we scrape it into the kitchen bin. Jordan says, "Let's make soil, Mommy!" We make a game of deciding what can and can't go in the bin. Now that I understand that microorganisms feeding on my table scraps are naturally producing nitrogen, potassium, and phosphorus to fertilize my soil, I delight in watching the leaves and vegetables break down. I love the earthy smell. I can't wait to feel the texture of the rich organic matter in my hands as I return these nutrients back to the earth so they can nourish my garden. I am in love with the whole process.

As a bonus, compost is cheap! You can make it simply with the yard and kitchen waste you might otherwise put in a plastic bag and send to a landfill. It makes so much sense!

For you braver souls, a Tupperware container inside the kitchen and compost heap outside can work just as well and will cost little. Finding instructions to start your own compost heap is just a Google search away. I particularly like the ones offered by Heidi Hunt, assistant editor of Mother Earth News (www.motherearthnews.com/Organic-Gardening/How-To-Start-A-Compost-Pile.aspx).

Nature Hiking Made Simple

This is one of those ideas that seemed like it should be intuitive until I actually set out to do it with my two-year-old boy and four-year-old girl. Here is some road-tested advice to maximize exposure to nature and security at the same time:

- Choose an appropriate venue to explore. If you have infants, very young children, or an elderly person accompanying you, consider a place with paved walking paths that offer places to rest and observe nature while sitting. Just because parks are paved does not disqualify them as nature hike options. There are still many chances to see flora and fauna along the way!

213

- Be as general or specific as you want. Perhaps you want to teach your kids about a particular rock formation, species of animal, or ecosystem. Or maybe you prefer to give your kids room to be inspired by whatever moves them. As long as you are teaching them to observe nature intentionally, something is bound to fascinate them.

- Safety is the most important consideration. Ensure the area does not have extreme drop-offs or deep water that pose perilous risks to toddlers running pell-mell. All that's needed is simple common sense and close supervision to let toddlers roam and enjoy nature hikes, keeping them safe and sound all the while.

- Pack a zero-waste picnic lunch. Bring food from home in reusable containers. Oranges, bananas, trail mix, and sandwiches are low maintenance, healthy, and easy to eat. Use the reusable containers to take home leftovers and add them to your compost.

- Bring a bag to tote home collectibles such as leaves, rocks, and flowers.

- For a virtual walk in the woods, check out http://urban ext.illinois.edu/woods. The interactive voice, beautiful pictures, and teacher's guide make this a great learning activity to share with your child.

Make Your Own Bird Feeders

This one is very easy and fun for ages three and up.

- Gather several sticks (8 to 12 inches long), several pieces of string or yarn (24 inches long), peanut butter, and birdseed.

- Tie a piece of string around one end of each stick to make a loop. Coat the other end of the stick in peanut butter. Spoon birdseed on top of the peanut butter end until it is fully coated. Help your child hang the sticks in a tree.

Green Websites Your Kids Will Love!

- National Geographic Kids (www.kids.nationalgeographic.com)—This is a great site where kids can blog, read stories, find activities, and look at pictures about wildlife and the planet.
- Tree of Life Web Project (www.tolweb.org)—This website is a collaborative collection of pictures, text, and other information about every species of organism, organized by biological classification system. This encyclopedic tool contains images, video files, presentations, lessons, and games about biodiversity.
- Encyclopedia of Life (www.eol.org)—This is another online tool that lists facts and pictures for every organism known to man.
- Kids Saving Energy (www.eere.energy.gov/kids)—Sponsored by the US Department of Energy, this is a user-friendly site to help kids (and grown-ups) of all ages learn about renewable energy and energy efficiency. On this site you'll find links to more than 350 lesson plans and activities on energy efficiency and renewable energy for grades K through 12.
- Adventures with Bobbie Bigfoot (www.kidsfootprint.org)—Kids can take an online ecological footprint quiz with Bobbie Bigfoot. Teachers and parents can also download free lesson plans.
- Friends for Change (http://tv.disney.go.com/disneychannel/friendsforchange/)—Disney's program lets kids make green pledges and vote for a variety of environmental projects for the company to fund.

- Identify bird species that are prevalent in your area. Print out pictures from an online search or use pictures from a field guide. Talk to your kids about birds they may expect to see eating from their feeders.

Calculate Your Family's Ecological Footprint

For a more cerebral activity, this is an excellent idea that my friend Dan uses on his fourth-grade class to show kids how many planets it takes and where the natural resources come from to support their families' lifestyles. This exercise is quick, user-friendly, and straightforward for kids and adults alike.

- Go to www.footprintnetwork.org. Under "Footprint Basics" on the top menu, select "Personal Footprint."

The quiz will let you create your own person. Engage your child in building the figure that will go through the exercise so he or she feels involved.

- At the end of the quiz, your lifestyle will be scored based on the number of planets it takes to support your choices. You'll also see the breakdown of global acres your family requires in terms of energy land, crop land, forest, grazing land, fishing grounds, and other factors. You can rerun different scenarios to see how you can reduce your impact.

- Now go to www.poodwaddle.com. Go to the Earth Clock. Your child will be amazed by watching this real-time clock count actual numbers for population growth, forest lost, forest replanted, oil used, species extinct, US trash produced, US trash recycled, and a number of other indicators. This makes for great discussion when your child really sees the actual impact your family can have by making positive changes.

Watch *WALL-E*

Since I opened this chapter with Disney, it's fitting I end it with Disney too. This idea is as straightforward as it gets, so I'll dispense with instructions. You and your kids will be moved by the story of WALL-E, a lovable solar-powered trash compactor left behind to deal with mountains of refuse after humans have evacuated the planet to live on a floating cruise ship in space. When WALL-E meets a robotic companion named EVE, he gives her his most precious possession, a single plant he found under all the trash. The story unfolds when EVE must return to the spaceship to deliver the plant to the humans, letting them know it's time to return home. Together they embark on an adventure to restore humans to the planet and Earth to its former splendor. It's a love story on so many levels.

PART 3

Being the Change

12

Green at Work

If your actions inspire others to dream more,
learn more, do more, and become more, you
are a leader.

John Quincy Adams,
6th president of the United States

Thus far, we've covered dozens of ways you can make a difference as a consumer, a citizen, a neighbor, and a parent. Still wondering what else you can do? Consider bringing your green mission to work. If you are looking around your workplace (this also goes for your school, church, or community) and no major green campaigns are under way, the role is just waiting to be filled.

But do you have the ability to influence people to change for the better? That part may take some doing. The key is having the willingness to learn new skills, either leadership skills to make positive changes at work, or new career skills to land a green job or build your own green business. As long as you have passion and a dedicated work ethic, you have the makings of a green leader.

From Executive Assistant to Green-Team Executive

Few companies outside the Fortune 1000 are going to fund a position for a full-time sustainability officer. However, companies of all sizes support voluntary employee-driven programs. Kimberly Logan is a great example of an employee who is successfully spearheading a voluntary green initiative. I met her when she hired me as a consultant to help her law firm, Strasburger and Price, to mobilize their newly formed green team. Wanting to know more about her motivations for taking on this voluntary role, I asked Kimberly to share her story with me.

"I was pursuing my business degree while working as an executive assistant," Kimberly explained. "For me, it was all business until I took an environmental elective. I did it just to get an easy A, but what I learned changed my life. They showed a video called *Not in My Backyard*. I'll never forget the images showing what we in the United States were doing with our trash. We were shipping it to a waste dump in Haiti. They've already got it bad, and now they get our trash? This video went on to discuss how we can change that by reusing, reducing, and recycling. It even said that businesses could save money by doing these things.

"When I went to work the next day and my managing partner asked me about my class, I told him what I learned," Kimberly said. "To my surprise, he asked me, 'What would you think about applying what you've learned in your environmental class to our company?' I told him, 'You know, I think I could do that.'"

Kimberly took the idea and ran with it. "I got on Google and started educating myself. I found a guide that talked about how to run a green team. It told me to begin with areas that wouldn't cost money." Kimberly started with evaluating the recycling system and the lighting in her building. "I called the building management company to see what they were doing. I asked our marketing director Susannah West to join me. We started looking at how we could reduce the energy we used. We began sending communications around the office, asking people to recycle their paper and to remember to turn off their lights. We gave them informational tips and factoids.

"Before we knew it, people were sending stuff back to us," Kimberly said. "We discovered pockets of people who were doing things on their own, like a group of secretaries toting home their bottles to recycle. In the process of all these conversations, more and more people became engaged. I would make notes and compile a committee of people who had replied to me. I went back to my boss, Dan, and told him about the interest. He said I could set up a committee."

Understanding the importance of having all levels of staff on board, Kimberly recruited partners to join the firm's green committee. For the first green-team meeting, she arranged a conference call for interested people from all five offices. "The turnout was amazing," she said. For the second meeting, Kimberly got approval to hire me to lead a motivational workshop to align all green-team members with the same goals and to create an action plan. Kimberly and Susannah had already done the legwork, creating a green mission statement and building team spirit. What they lacked was a definitive road map with goals and milestones. I helped them draft an action plan and encouraged them to support the ABA-EPA Law Office Climate Challenge, a special program for law offices sponsored by ENERGY STAR in partnership with the American Bar Association. As a result of Kimberly's leadership, all five offices are participating in this program.

I asked Kimberly if there have been any challenges. "People never run out of good ideas, but they won't always sign up to execute them," she said. "You have to grow a thick skin to lead a team. I'm glad I asked them to sign commitment forms at the beginning, because now I have permission to hold them accountable." Kimberly got into this leadership role out of personal conviction, but she's finding as she grows into it that not everyone is propelled by the same level of enthusiasm as she is. "You have to follow up. It can get a little discouraging. I manage those feelings by continuing to keep the lines of communication open." She added, "I think it would be great if people's efforts could be measured through professional development evaluations or incentives. Everyone needs praise when they're doing valuable work."

Hearing this, I am touched on so many levels. One person cared enough to create a documentary to educate viewers about a sad reality going on in Haiti. One teacher cared enough to show the film during a class. One person cared enough to share with her boss what she had learned in her class. One boss cared enough to empower that employee to make a plan. An entire company became greener because of a small chain of people who ask the simple question, "What can I do to make a difference?"

I told Kimberly that I'm proud of her company, but I'm even prouder of her. It isn't easy being a single person setting out to change a group. "I have learned so much through this process," she told me. "I am closer to my co-workers than before. I have a stronger voice within the company now. The personal growth alone has been worth it." When you set out to improve the world, you can't help but improve yourself too.

Turn Work into Play with Green Promo Products

A subtle and inexpensive way to inject some eco-friendliness into your organization is through recycled promotional products. Buy customized biodegradable pens, organic tees, newspaper visors, mouse pads made from old tires, or coasters made from recycled circuit boards for your next office picnic, conference, or employee motivation day— or every day.

My favorite supplier is Weisenbach Specialty Printing and Manufacturing, a twenty-five-year-old, Ohio-based green products veteran. Visit www.recycledproducts.com for an online catalog featuring more than 600 products.

How to Create Change in a Conservative Culture

If sustainability makes sense, why isn't everyone doing it? The hurdle is not the hard facts as much as the soft ones. Organizations, like people, have personalities. Some are progressive, but most are conservative. When it comes to sustainability, the progressives get a lot of press, but in reality, they are the exceptions to the rule. Conservatives are cautious; progressives throw caution to the wind. Conservatives are grounded in reality; progressives are planted in possibility. Although these are broad generalizations, in today's highly charged political environment, any issue, particularly a heated one such as energy, is subject to sweeping generalizations and half-truths.

So how do we chart a course for change within a conservative culture without being labeled as progressive—and potentially disregarded as a result? That question was on my mind when I met Dan Northcutt, the director of environmental studies at St. Mark's School of Texas, a private preparatory school for boys. Dan has been with St. Mark's for over twenty years. In fact, if you count the six years he spent there as a student, you could say he's been there for nearly thirty years. During that time Dan has seen a lot. He remembers the late seventies when conserving energy was considered patriotic. To do their part, those at the school removed every other bulb from the light fixtures in hallways and classrooms. Then came the 1980s, and the zeal for energy conservation in America waned. Nearly two decades of relatively cheap energy followed. But thanks in part to Dan's efforts, conservation is once again a priority for the school.

During the past two years, St. Mark's has implemented a single-stream recycling program and has switched its power source to a blend of 30 percent renewable energy, setting a goal to increase that amount by 10 percent each year. Dan's AP environmental science elective is so popular that the school added a second section. An environmental component is also being integrated into the curriculum of the lower school, giv-

What Qualities Should a Green Leader Cultivate?

Although Dan Northcutt has a longer history in his organization than the typical employee, longevity has less to do with his success than the vital qualities of personal commitment, a penchant for education, a collaborative approach, and sheer enthusiasm. The green programs that gain traction, when compared to the ones that produce lackluster results, are created through one person or team exhibiting these traits:

1. **Personal commitment.** As the director of environmental studies, Dan demonstrates knowledge of ecology and conservation on a daily basis. He also walks his own talk by living a green lifestyle. No one is suspicious of his motives.

2. **Education.** Conservatives don't want people selling to them, but they do want to be informed. What tends to hold people back, even CEOs, from jumping into new territory are concerns that they can't quite articulate. People need to develop a comfort level with green ideas. For the headmaster, Dan created a "green print" plan, prioritizing and budgeting every element of his strategy. Dan engages the students through his environmental science classes, the administration through practical modifications for a greener campus, the parents through newsletters, and the community through free events such as movie festivals featuring eco-oriented documentaries.

3. **Collaboration.** Dan is just one guy. As with any organization, St. Mark's has multiple spheres of influence: students, parents, administrators, and board members. By working with these groups to address their specific concerns or interests, Dan is not pushing an agenda but providing a service. He's garnering support throughout the process by asking influential people for help with these programs.

4. **Enthusiasm.** Dan has fun. He likes people and seeks to understand them. Dan's persistence is tempered by his enthusiasm, so that even when he urges people to make green changes, he does so without annoying them. Enthusiasm is the antidote to burnout for anyone steering a green initiative inside a change-resistant culture.

ing younger students exposure to sustainability concepts at an early age. Even the teachers' lounge reflects eco-consciousness, now that Styrofoam cups have been replaced with ceramic mugs bearing St. Mark's special green branding.

The most significant reflection of St. Mark's commitment is the board of trustees' approval of LEED certification for its two new buildings. This decision added just 2 percent more to the construction cost, which St. Mark's will recover within approximately ten years—less if the cost of energy rises—with the added benefit of a healthier indoor environment. The school's eco-improvements, which began two decades ago with Dan, now have the support of teachers, administration, students, parents, and the board. How one person helped drive change at St. Mark's presents a road map any green leader can follow.

To drive progress in a conservative culture, you must demonstrate the following:

1. **Top-level support.** While a progressive culture will take grassroots efforts seriously, a conservative culture is more likely to follow the direction of top-level leadership. When St. Mark's board of trustees decided that building its new facilities to LEED standards was the right thing to do, the school's green program finally got some teeth. Sustainability went from being "Dan's project" to becoming a core value of the organization.

2. **Management-level and administrative support.** A major stumbling block in organizations that fulfill the first prerequisite is failure to engage other rungs of employees. Engaging stakeholders requires a sincere statement backed by action on the part of the leader, as well as education and incentives to motivate staff that may be reticent to support "progressive" ideas.

3. **Minimal risk.** Any initiative perceived as a risk to the culture's brand or product will not gain support.

4. **A clear path.** Conservative cultures are not innovative by nature. By sharing case studies of similar companies' sustainability initiatives, change agents can offer a concrete path to follow. Reputable third-party certifications such as ENERGY STAR offer a step-by-step plan as well as promotional materials and opportunities for recognition.

5. **Bottom-line value.** The numbers have to demonstrate a relatively short payback period with a clear return on investment.

6. **Political awareness.** Know the culture. I had to learn this lesson the hard way. Sometimes you can have everything else in place and the plan can still fall flat. Never underestimate the importance of hierarchy in the planning stage. Know your audience. If you don't engage the right people early on, they will not appreciate the value of a sustainability plan that may require funds or behavioral changes, even if the numbers work on paper.

Conservation is still a conservative value, so why the push back from conservative cultures? The reality is that most companies, like people, don't make decisions according to their values as much as their circumstances, especially in uncertain times. In this case, green leaders might dispense with idealism and try Dan's pragmatic approach, which he succinctly summarized in the words of Harry Truman: "It's amazing what you can accomplish if you don't care who gets the credit."[1]

Leading a Green Team

As an outside consultant, I cannot change an entire organization, no matter the size. I've learned to tell clients this up front, as they seem to expect change to happen on its own after a single workshop or even a three-month project. If it were that easy, our world wouldn't be in the situation it is right now! Most of what I do is find someone motivated on the inside, like Dan Northcutt or Kimberly Logan, and empower that person with resources, tools, and coaching to cover every aspect of a green program.

Whether I'm speaking to the CEO or to the executive assistant, I hear the same question: "Where do we start?" No matter who is asking, I present the same model. In order to implement a successful green program, organizations must address five key areas: people, facilities, operations, products, and brand. Organizations that consistently address these areas, measure them, and invest time and resources into them will have the most success. While no green-team leader will have full authority over all (or any) of these areas, he or she needs to understand the relevance each area has to a profitable green strategy.

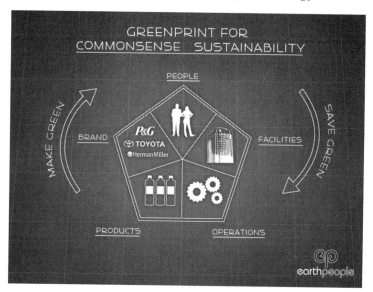

1. People

Everything starts with people. An organization's most valuable resources are its human ones. People are the heart and soul of a good sustainability strategy. Employees from all levels and interest groups need to be aligned with the program. Many excellent guides exist that can help you guide and empower your green team, no matter your role in your organization. Here are a few:

- "Bring Your Green to Work" and "Guidelines for Energy Management" from ENERGY STAR (www.energystar.gov)
- "Working 9 to 5 on Climate Change" from World Resources Institute (www.wri.org/publication/content/8361)
- "A Guide to Greening Your Bottom Line Through a Resource-Efficient Office Environment" from the City of

227

Portland Office of Sustainable Development (www.oregon
.gov/energy/cons/bus/docs/Green_Office_Guide.pdf)
- "Green Office Toolkit" from Jones Lang LaSalle (www.
joneslanglasalle.com/microsites/GreenOfficeToolkit)
- *Profiting from Green Business*, a free e-book from my
website (www.annamclark.com/books).

2. Facilities

CFO magazine reports that 75 percent of business leaders
think that energy costs are the least controllable cost in business.
This is simply not the case. You can exercise control over your
energy costs through energy efficiency. Even small changes can
lead to big returns: IBM saved $17.8 million worldwide in one
year just by encouraging employees to turn out the lights.

Even if your company leases space, lighting retrofits can be
worthwhile if you're a long-term lessee. One of my clients, a
corporate tenant leasing 200,000 square feet in a downtown
office building, found that up to $89,000 per year could be
saved on energy costs with the installation of compact fluorescent lighting. With seven years remaining on their lease
and a payback period of only two years, the company could
save over $400,000 for the term of the lease.

The ENERGY STAR website (www.energystar.gov) is rife
with success stories of small and midsize companies that have
retrofitted their facilities with energy-efficient features, recover-
ing their investment within one to three years and saving tens
of thousands of dollars per year on operating costs. ENERGY
STAR also offers promotional materials and marketing tools
enabling people to promote energy efficiency to stakeholders.

3. Operations

You enter the building of a company and are seated in the
waiting area. An employee offers you one of two beverages:
bottled water or coffee in a Styrofoam cup. Right off the bat,
it's harder to think of that company as green. Now magnify
that across the board for all the products used within that

company's offices and manufacturing facilities. What about their waste and their water usage? A company's internal operations and external vendors are a reflection of core business values. This is the area that requires the most work but can be a major source of savings and quality improvement. Outside consulting firms such as EarthPeople can help companies reduce CO_2 emissions, energy use, materials use, and waste by evaluating the supply chain and other internal processes. The aforementioned guides can help green teams determine a scope for their project and perform some basic assessments before hiring a professional.

4. Products

Companies that want to incorporate sustainability into product design have many choices. One method I like for manufacturers and nonmanufacturers alike is the Natural Step Framework (NSF), which is being used successfully around the world by leading business, government, academic, and religious institutions and individuals to build healthier environments, save money, reduce waste, improve performance, gain strategic position, eliminate regulatory burdens, and build teams. According to independent NSF instructor Terry Gips, "It all happens by learning how to apply a set of principles to any process, guaranteeing a more sustainable outcome." While product innovation lies outside the domain of most employees, your green team can still brainstorm and submit ideas to your company's leadership. You may be more influential than you think.

5. Brand

Companies that have a comprehensive green strategy in place should not hesitate to share their eco-accomplishments with their stakeholders. I tell clients that each point of contact with the company represents an opportunity to attract green-minded customers and increase brand value through green messaging (provided it is backed up with substantive sustainability efforts). Try working with your marketing department to find the best way to vocalize your company's green achievements. Options for communicating green initiatives include:

- Advertising
- Annual report
- Business partners and vendors
- Community relations
- Corporate offices
- Customer word of mouth
- Employees
- Marketing collateral
- Media relations
- Shareholders
- Signage
- Sponsorships
- Thought leadership
- Website

Getting a Green-Collar Job

If you want to make helping the planet your full-time job, consider a "green-collar" career. Green-collar workers install solar panels, retrofit buildings to make them more efficient, construct transit lines, refine waste oil into biodiesel, erect wind farms, repair hybrid cars, build green rooftops, plant trees, and so much more. Some of them are next-generation blue-collar jobs; others are white-collar professional opportunities in sustainability, sales, training, communications, and other roles related to corporate social responsibility and sustainability.

So how can you smartly plunge into the green-collar job market? SustainLane Media CEO James Elsen, who recently launched a green-job board on his site, is already attracting more than one hundred listings each week across several industries. Elsen offers sound advice for people trying to break into this field: "Don't worry about starting at the bottom. You're never going to have another opportunity in your career where the bottom is so close to the top. Someone with three years of solar experience right now is a foremost expert in the country!" Putting this into perspective, Elsen continues, "We're about to experience the greatest renaissance in product development that we've ever seen in our lifetime. For every job like a photovoltaic engineer, there are eight to ten jobs needed to support that. Some people have anxieties about entering a new industry, but it's also very exciting. It's a thrilling place to be, if you like to learn. In terms of getting job training, we hear so much about four-year schools, but really community colleges have some of the best opportunities for retraining and job skills."[2]

If you are having trouble finding the green job of your dreams, consider creating one. Become a green entrepreneur, or "eco-preneur." I've made friends in every field who are building successful businesses around ideas to make the world a better place. This is not for the faint of heart, but it can certainly be done with research, commitment, a good idea, a willingness to learn as you go, and lots of elbow grease. Like

Green-Collar Career Center

Websites are springing up all over the place to help with finding a green job. Here are a few:

Greenbiz.com Jobs (http://jobs.greenbiz.com)
Green Jobs (www.greenjobs.com)
Green Jobs Network (www.greenjobs.net)
Sustainable Business Green Dream Jobs (www.sustainablebusiness.com/index.cfm/go/greendreamjobs.main)
SustainLane (www.sustainlane.com/green-jobs)
Treehugger Job Board (http://jobs.treehugger.com)

If you are passionate about promoting the cause of fostering a green-collar workforce, consider supporting these organizations:

Green for All (www.greenforall.org)
Green Jobs Now (www.greenjobsnow.com)

Thomas Edison said, "Opportunity is missed by most people because it is dressed in overalls and looks like work." Or my personal favorite: "There are no rules here—we're trying to accomplish something."

If we did all the things we are capable of, we would literally astound ourselves.

Thomas Edison, American inventor, scientist, and businessman

If you do choose to start your own business, don't expect the path to be straight and narrow. On the road to building your dream green business, you might have to endure a few side trips. When I left IBM in 2003 to venture into the world of entrepreneurship, I had to navigate new territory without the skills I would need to sell a concept, set up operations, or secure funding. Not surprisingly, the dream for my first company ended when the reality hit that I would need $70,000 just to start it. (As it turns out, importing furniture from Indonesia wasn't my calling anyway.) So what did I do instead? I bought a $100 starter kit for a business with Mary Kay Cosmetics. Taking an unconventional path ended up being a blessing. Sitting behind a desk and playing it safe could not have given me the experience Mary Kay offered in terms of leadership, public speaking, marketing, bookkeeping, and, most importantly, sales. It turned out to be the ultimate growth experience.

Most people live and die with their music still unplayed. They never dare to try.

Mary Kay Ash, founder of multi-billion-dollar cosmetics empire

After three years of intentionally acquiring the necessary entrepreneurial skills—and unintentionally earning a pink Cadillac—I was ready to forgo my pink business (and pink car) for a greener one. Since founding EarthPeople in 2005, I've been a green-business pioneer by helping people and companies find their own niche in the green space. Up or down, it's been worth the ride.

13

Finding Your Voice

We must be the change we wish to see in the world.

Mahatma Gandhi, civil rights leader

So you've come this far, have you? If you've read this book in full, you know more about what it takes to build a sustainable society than 99 percent of Americans. Even if you look around and think it's already being done, the record shows that much more must happen if we are to solve this crisis. We need to reduce emissions by 2 percent each year to reach the necessary 80 percent reduction by 2050, but we are still increasing emissions at a rate of 11 percent each year. We are moving backwards. It's time to get off the sidelines. Our country needs your voice!

One person can make a difference, and it doesn't take a lifetime to do it. If you don't yet believe this, consider my story. In 2005, I knew next to nothing about green living. In fact, other than good intentions, I was one of the least green people you could find. After taking the journey I've described in this book, I've become a more conscientious consumer and a more educated voter. I've reduced my family's environmental footprint significantly. I've also built a company helping green businesses gain the credibility required to be competitive. By 2008, I was on my way to publishing my first book. And in 2009, my company, EarthPeople, went worldwide. Our consulting firm has developed strategic partnerships in South Africa and Australia, giving us a global platform. Our clients include municipalities such as Austin, schools such as Columbia University, and brands such as *Fortune* magazine. Our work includes everything from designing green jeans to promoting clean vehicle technology. Where else but in the green space can someone move so quickly from neophyte to expert? It's less a testament to luck or skill than sheer enthusiasm for teaching people the very ideas I was so eager to learn myself.

Like I said at the beginning of this book, there is no lack of information out there when it comes to going green. What we still lack are enough people with the will to take these ideas and run with them. Leadership—personal responsibility on a larger scale—is the quality that built America, and it's the quality that can save it too.

Are you itching to start a discussion group, lead a green team, launch a green website, find a green job, join a green club, write a green book, organize a green event, start an organic garden, or try any of the other ideas in this book? If you want to, intend to, mean to . . . but still don't know how to, then your problem isn't that you don't have enough information; it's that you don't have enough experience. Experience is gained by taking one step at a time, making mistakes, falling down, getting back up, and continuing on. If you get started now, before you know it you'll look up and discover that you're taking others with you. That's all it takes to be a leader.

The Butterfly Trap

I've been learning a lot from nature since I opened my eyes to it again. Take a butterfly, for instance. Until recently, my primary exposure to the act of metamorphosis was through reading Eric Carle's *The Very Hungry Caterpillar* to my daughter. "One Sunday morning the warm sun came up and—pop!— out of the egg came a tiny and very hungry caterpillar."[1] It turns out the real process isn't quite so easy.

The caterpillar stays in its cocoon, called a chrysalis, until it is ready to emerge. During this period, which can range from several weeks to several months depending on the species, the pupal wings undergo rapid mitosis and absorb a great deal of nutrients. A newly emerged butterfly needs to spend some time inflating its wings with blood and letting them dry, during which time it is extremely vulnerable to predators. Before the butterfly gets its wings, it must suffer exposure, vulnerability, and danger.

> *There is nothing in a caterpillar that tells you it's going to be a butterfly.*
>
> R. Buckminster Fuller, American architect, inventor, and futurist

When we observe the butterfly, we never see that slimy, shivering larvae trying to pump itself up. All we see is the magnificence of its color-drenched wings. We admire the beauty of the end result, while we ignore the in-between that made it happen. By focusing only on the butterfly, we neglect the vast potential in the caterpillar. I call this phenomenon the "butterfly trap"—the misguided belief that only some are special enough to fly while the rest of us must be content to creep.

I think butterfly lore is so prevalent in art and literature because humans are fascinated by transformation. We love the idea of coming into our own, of being glorious. We admire people who are famous or accomplished. We may even wish we could be like them. And yet, we're afraid to shed our cocoons, to be vulnerable, to change, and to risk looking stupid—all of which are necessary steps to personal growth. The good news is that metamorphosis only looks like magic. In reality, it is a methodical process that anyone can emulate.

235

Apart from getting to be a kid again and rediscovering the beauty of the natural world, my greatest joy in this work has been watching ordinary people do extraordinary things. I believe that, above all else, people are a renewable resource. Any one of us can learn the traits of influence and perseverance that set those who succeed apart from the rest. Why leave all the world-changing opportunities to the "natural-born leaders" when you can become a natural-*grown* leader instead?

> *The caterpillar does all the work but the butterfly gets all the publicity.*
>
> George Carlin, comedian

A Better Life, a Better World

Is your cocoon keeping you from pursuing your plan? Finding your voice is like growing a pair of wings. It begins quietly and with a lot of nourishment. It is not something you have to do in front of an audience, although you may find yourself doing that someday too. Once you get started, you will look around and begin to recognize others who are going through the same thing. You may not know for a while where the process is taking you, but there is no doubt about where it's taking you from. Get ready to shed that cocoon. It's time to grow a pair! (Of wings, naturally.)

You can decide to have a quiet voice of conviction by making a difference within your own home, or you can choose a louder voice by educating other people. I've had so much experience with this process personally and through coaching others that I've fairly well mapped it out. The system I've created is called Natural-Grown Leader. Though growing a platform for leadership lies outside the scope of this chapter, I will close with the five most important steps for bursting out of your cocoon and finding your voice. Prepare to make a difference right now, right where you are.

1. Indulge in Nature Therapy

In 2005 I could no longer stand it. I couldn't read one more article about melting sea ice and drowning walruses without doing something, anything. But what? Searching for clarity, I started going to the Dallas Arboretum, a wonderful park near my house filled with trees, meadows, streams, and exotic flowers (although anywhere scenic would have worked). I brought a pen and paper to help me unscramble my thoughts. Out of that came my first children's stories and eventually a business plan for my company. I can't tell you how it happened, except that it did. Once I regained my lost connection with nature, my creativity came rushing back.

Call it nature therapy. We humans are part of nature. We draw oxygen, sustenance, energy, optimism, hope, and peace from dwelling in it. If you find that you don't have those things, run to a park or some lovely place and just sit and soak it up. It will open your mind, leading you to ideas you never knew you had.

2. Find a Mentor (or Five)

Nature can't thrive in a vacuum. Where would the flowers and birds be without the bees? Humans can't thrive in a vacuum either. You don't have to be a social butterfly to know that we are fundamentally social creatures. I think that is what's driving the explosion of social-media websites: a lot of people dying to have a voice have now found one. The problem is, we're drowning each other out. How do you cultivate a voice that will rise above the din? You cannot find your voice if you don't have anyone to talk to.

Only through connecting with others and listening to their voices have I been able to refine my own. So how did I go from reading someone else's words to writing them? I did it by finding the right mentors.

I am not a self-made person. My voice has been shaped by thousands of others: readers, bloggers, listeners, and mentors.

My first mentor was Ann Drumm, the chair of the Dallas chapter of the Sierra Club. Ann showed me the ropes in terms of activism and community outreach. Once I created my business plan, I reached out to Terry Gips, a sustainability expert in Minnesota with over twenty years of experience. We've still never met in person, yet he has been a huge motivator for me. So has Dan Weisenbach, a recycled-products manufacturer in Ohio who has generously shared his time and experience with me.

> "Just living is not enough," said the butterfly, "one must have sunshine, freedom, and a little flower."
>
> Hans Christian Andersen,
> Danish author and poet

As I got further into my work, I realized I wasn't going to be able to avoid public speaking. I also realized I couldn't avoid writing. Christine Cashen, a dynamic motivational speaker I knew through a friend, became my speaking mentor. And through my friend Anna's networking function, I met writer and PR extraordinaire Nancy Lowell. By chance, Nancy asked if I would like a writing lesson. She sat with me for two hours to help me write out my first letter to the editor: a fifty-word blurb on recycling. A few months later I was writing articles. A few years later I was writing books.

Not one of these people ever asked me to pay them for their help, and yet they've become a de facto advisory board—not to mention my friends. I'm adding mentors all the time, especially when there is something new I want to learn.

3. Be a Teacher

You don't need a classroom full of students to be a teacher. One is all it takes to make a difference. Think of Helen Keller's teacher Anne Sullivan. Through the support of one woman, Helen Keller gained the communication skills to influence the entire world, and Anne Sullivan gained an extraordinary friendship and legacy. What a difference we could all make if we took a fraction of Sullivan's commitment in sharing our knowledge with others.

My first foray into teaching happened when I took on my first intern, Chrissy Runyan. Chrissy and I met in a sustainability discussion group hosted by the Sierra Club. Chrissy was enthusiastic about my idea for EarthPeople, and she wanted to learn about consulting. Not only did I enjoy teaching her about my work, but I also found the experience made learning more fun for me too. Chrissy, who went on to study environmental science at Johns Hopkins and then pursued a PhD at the University of Virginia, now acts as an advisor to EarthPeople. She also remains my greatest cheerleader. That's the beauty of teaching someone else—you gain more than you give.

> *We delight in the beauty of the butterfly, but rarely admit the changes it has gone through to achieve that beauty.*
>
> Maya Angelou, American poet

It's been even more wonderful to teach my children. Watching the movie *Arctic Tale* with my four-year-old daughter, Jordan, I told her gently about the melting of the sea ice—the habitat for our favorite animals. It didn't take long before Jordan was warning me to turn out the lights, "because it helps the polar bears and the walruses!" And when she finishes a banana, she says, "Mommy, let's compost the peel." Of all the teaching any of us can do to save the planet, it's the little lessons (and people) that can end up making the biggest difference.

4. Find Your Niche

There is no job description for "environmental inspirer." How could there be? I made it up, but not to satisfy my vanity, to make a pile of money, or to look good. In fact, my experience in the first few years was the opposite of those rewards, and

239

I'm still growing into the role. Anyone expecting an immediate windfall for going green better keep on moving. You go green for the sheer joy of making a difference. If you stay committed, saving money or making money is inevitable. Finding a niche for your skills and interests will help your green hobby, green project, or green career become a more successful endeavor.

I found my niche unexpectedly. I was doing a life purpose exercise in Jack Canfield's book *Success Principles*. Without a clue as to what would result, I went through the exercise and out came my mission statement: "To inspire and educate others to care about the natural world." What was I supposed to do with that? I was in leadership with Mary Kay at the time, driving a pink Cadillac, no less. How was I supposed to get from there to here? I set the paper aside, but it never left my thoughts.

A month later I attended a spiritual gifts retreat at my church. After doing the exercises, we were told to draw a picture of what we thought our work should look like. Mine looked like a stick figure speaking to a lot of other stick figures, with pictures of wind turbines, flowers, and sunshine all over the place. It was a crude drawing of the mission statement I had created. I decided to listen this time.

To say my mission found me would be ignoring the fact that I worked so hard to find it. Doing some soul-searching and setting realistic goals will help you funnel your time into worthwhile tasks that bear fruit.

5. Be Okay with Looking Stupid

We humans have a tendency to dismiss the ugly ducklings while we swoon over the swans, those self-assured creatures who have already reached their zenith. As a result, many of us work hard to improve the way something looks to the rest of the world, while ignoring the voice inside that tells us where we're really meant to go. Who is behind that voice? Somebody much more important than those people we're trying to impress.

If you truly want to accomplish something great, you are going to have to leave your comfort zone. You may as well get comfortable being uncomfortable, at least for a while. Most of us would prefer anything over feeling awkward or embarrassed. I know because as a shy child, I felt that way all the time until I hit age twenty. There are times when I still feel it. The solution is to feel the fear and do something great anyway.

I had a head start in overcoming fear before green ever registered on my radar. Resigning from IBM to start a career at the bottom with Mary Kay was an exercise in getting over myself. Talk about busting out of my cocoon and hanging myself out there to dry! Every day for three years I put myself in front of strangers, inviting them to try my product or consider my opportunity. But for that experience, I would not be doing the same thing today with CEOs on a bigger stage with a bigger mission.

As formative as my previous experience had been, when I decided to become a sustainability expert I had to start all over again. Speaking to a roomful of executives about green business was a whole new ball game. Talk about knocking knees and a quivering voice. My first speaking engagement was a disaster. I droned on for forty-five minutes when I should have kept it to twenty. People were shifting in their seats, but I kept on until I'd read all the points in my outline. I wish I could say it got better after that, but it took several years to become polished and focused enough to learn how to communicate my ideas effectively without using notes. But what else is a green pioneer to do? I assure you that you can get over feeling stupid and come out stronger than before. But first you have to get started.

Now Do Something!

The green advantage offers opportunities for people from all walks of life. I recently participated in an interdisciplinary roundtable discussion among people in fields related to the environment. We all convened for the purpose of fostering a more sustainable community by sharing our knowledge, personal journeys, and networking. Among those at the table were an organic farmer, an environmental health expert, a corporate sustainability executive, a community organizer, an assistant city manager, a sustainable developer, a nonprofit executive director, a judge, a scientist, a poet, a writer, several teachers, and others. As a cross-section of our society, the group reflected the breadth and depth of ways that sustainability connects all of us. Every one of us at the table, no matter our backgrounds, admitted to figuring things out as we went along.

> *I do not know whether I was then a man dreaming I was a butterfly, or whether I am now a butterfly dreaming I am a man.*
>
> Chuang Tzu, ancient
> Chinese philosopher

Environmental stewardship is nothing more than doing what comes naturally. If we really think about it, aren't health, financial opportunity, national security, and our children's future important to us all? Wouldn't most people try to make the world a better place if they just believed they could? Not everyone needs a public platform to inspire others to care for our planet. A small vegetable patch will do.

No matter which end of the spectrum you find yourself on at the present moment, greener living is not a destination; it's a journey. I'm so glad you decided to join me.

Discussion Questions

Part 1: The Next American Revolution

1. A major theme in chapter 1 is how difficult it is in today's media-steeped culture to receive unbiased, factual information rather than biased opinion. Do you think the media has made people more capable of independent thought, or less? Do you think the media is skewed? If so, why?

2. What effect does it have on you to know that America is experiencing an epidemic in obesity while 800 million people in the world are suffering from hunger and starvation?

3. Former president George W. Bush said, "America is addicted to oil." For forty years our country has lacked a comprehensive energy policy. What do you think are the barriers to creating such a policy? Do you feel like you are participating as much in the political process as you could? If not, why not?

4. Chapter 2 describes eight major reasons why the green movement is gaining momentum: human rights, energy insecurity, globalization, population growth, habitat

destruction, climate change, water scarcity, and health hazards. With so many compelling reasons to take action, why do you think so many people get stuck in the climate-change argument? What arguments for going green resonate the most with you?

5. Do you see green changes happening in the companies that you buy from or support with your investment dollars? Have you thought about trying to influence them toward greater environmental responsibility?

6. In his book *Serve God, Save the Planet*, Matthew Sleeth describes what it was like to leave his position as a chief of staff in his hospital and move his family into a house the size of their former garage. According to his family, their journey toward simplicity has been full of unexpected blessings. What did you think about their story? Can you ever see yourself wanting to try something like that?

7. What do you think about environmental stewardship as a means to exercise your faith? Do you have any ideas you would like to try to introduce this topic into your faith community?

Part 2: 85 Easy Ways to Save the Planet (and Money!)

1. Chapter 5 defines affluenza as "an epidemic of stress, overwork, waste, and indebtedness caused by the pursuit of the American Dream." As you look around, do you see a problem with affluenza in our society? What do you think is behind this?

2. Have you ever felt the urge to simplify your life? What is keeping you from doing it? Be honest!

3. What are your obstacles to greener grocery shopping? What can you do to add more organic foods and/or vegetarian recipes to your diet? Do you have some favorite recipes you could share with friends?

4. Voting with your dollars is a big theme in this book. Have you purchased a great green product that you would like to endorse? If not, are you contemplating a green purchase, such as a car?

5. After reading about the toxic substances common in our personal-care products, have you taken an inventory of ingredients in your own products? Do you have a new green product that you would recommend to someone you know?

6. Have you undertaken any green remodeling projects in your home? What would prevent you from switching to a green power provider and/or installing compact fluorescent lightbulbs (CFLs)?

7. Do you think a community garden is a possibility in your neighborhood? If not, why not? What about growing your own garden at home?

8. What are some activities that you like to do with your kids to promote conservation? Share your ideas and experiences with other parents.

Part 3: Being the Change

1. Are you participating in any green projects at work, school, or your place of worship? If so, has it gone as expected? If not, what has gone wrong?

2. What aspects about leadership scare you? What is preventing you from doing more at work or even in your home to make the world a better place?

3. What are three green goals you would like to accomplish after reading this book?

Notes

Introduction

1. The Dictionary of Sustainable Management, http://www.sustainabilitydic tionary.com/s/sustainability.php.

2. 10news.com, "Americans Consume an Astounding Amount," April 22, 2008, http://www.10news.com/news/15961429/detail.html.

3. The Hawaii Association for Marine Education and Research, Inc., "State of Our Planet," http://www.hamerinhawaii.org/Main%20Web%20Pages/Education/ State%20of%20the%20Planet/ten_shocking_facts_planet.htm.

Chapter 1: Eco-Mania: The Truth behind the Hype

1. 100 People: A World Portrait, http://www.100people.org/statistics_100stats .php?section=statistics.

2. American Obesity Association, "Obesity in the US," May 2, 2005, http:// obesity1.tempdomainname.com/subs/fastfacts/obesity_US.shtml.

3. Johns Hopkins Bloomberg School of Public Health, "Study Suggests 86 Percent of Americans Could Be Overweight or Obese by 2030," July 28, 2008, http://www. jhsph.edu/publichealthnews/press_releases/2008/wang_obesity_projections.

4. Paul R. Ehrlich and Anne H. Ehrlich, "Too Many People, Too Much Consumption," *Yale Environment 360*, August 4, 2008, http://e360.yale.edu/content/ feature.msp?id=2041.

5. Margaret Mitchell, *Gone with the Wind* (Norwalk: Easton Press, 1996), 94.

6. Sterling A. Brown, *The Book of American Negro Poetry*, ed. James Weldon Johnson (New York: Harcourt, Brace, 1931).

7. *Gone with the Wind*, DVD, directed by David O'Selznick (Los Angeles: Metro-Goldwyn-Mayer, 1939).

8. Christopher Uhl, *Developing Ecological Consciousness: Paths to a Sustainable Future* (Lanham, MD: Rowman & Littlefield, 2003), 322.

9. *Gone with the Wind*, DVD.

Chapter 2: The Roots of a Green Revolution

1. Lamar Graham, "The Greenest Town in America," *Parade*, April 19, 2009, 8.

2. The United States Conference of Mayors, "US Conference of Mayors Climate Protection Agreement," 2008, http://www.usmayors.org/climateprotection/agreement.htm.

3. *The Green Bible* (New York: HarperCollins, 2008), I-37.

4. David Seidenberg, "Human Rights and Ecology—A Jewish Magazine, an Interfaith Movement," *Tikkun*, July/August 2008, http://www.tikkun.org/article.php/DavidSeidenberg-Humanrightsandecology.

5. John Vidal and Tom Kington, "Protect God's Creation: Vatican Issues New Green Message for World's Catholics," *Guardian*, April 27, 2007, http://www.guardian.co.uk/world/2007/apr/27/catholicism.religion.

6. James Woolsey, "The Long War of the 21st Century: How We Must Fight It" (speech, Southern Methodist University, Dallas, TX, October 7, 2005).

7. MSNBC, "Study: ANWR Oil Would Have Little Impact," March 16, 2004, http://www.msnbc.msn.com/id/4542853.

8. Jonathan Ablett, Aadarsh Baijal, Eric Beinhocker, Anupam Bose, Diana Farrell, and Ulrich Gersch, "The Bird of Gold: The Rise of India's Consumer Market," McKinsey Global Institute, May 2007, http://www.mckinsey.com/mgi/publications/India_consumer_market/index.asp.

9. Al Gore, *An Inconvenient Truth* (Emmaus, PA: Rodale, 2007), 216.

10. Edward O. Wilson, *The Future of Life* (New York: Vintage Books, 2002), 33.

11. Physorg.com, "Reef Sharks Threatened by Overfishing," December 5, 2006, http://www.physorg.com/news84538148.html.

12. Science Daily, "Extinction Rate across the Globe Reaches Historical Proportions," January 10, 2002, http://www.sciencedaily.com/releases/2002/01/020109074801.htm.

13. ZSL Institute of Zoology, "Biodiversity Plummeting," May 16, 2008, http://www.zsl.org/science/news/biodiversity-plummeting,458,NS.html.

14. Anne Penketh, "Appeal: In Mali, Villagers Have to Walk Miles to Fetch Water. And Then Drinking It May Kill Them," *The Independent World*, December 8, 2004, http://www.independent.co.uk/news/world/africa/appeal-in-mali-villagers-have-to-walk-miles-to-fetch-water-and-then-drinking-it-may-kill-them-679917.html.

15. Mark Clayton, "Is Water Becoming 'the New Oil'?" *Christian Science Monitor*, May 29, 2008, http://features.csmonitor.com/environment/2008/05/29/is-water-becoming-%E2%80%98the-new-oil%E2%80%99.

16. Ibid.

17. Wyland Foundation with Steve Creech, *Hold Your Water!* (Kansas City, MO: Andrews McMeel Publishing, 2006), xviii.

18. Clayton, "Is Water Becoming 'the New Oil'?"

19. Our Stolen Future, "The Bottom Line," http://www.ourstolenfuture.com/Basics/bottomline.htm.

20. Theo Colborn, Dianne Dumanoski, and John Peterson Myers, *Our Stolen Future* (New York: Penguin, 1997), 196.
   21. Science Daily, "EPA Ozone Pollution Standards 'Unhealthy for America,' Says American Thoracic Society President," June 22, 2007, http://www.sciencedaily.com/releases/2007/06/070621143648.htm.
   22. American Academy of Allergy, Asthma, and Immunology, "Asthma Statistics," http://www.aaaai.org/media/resources/media_kit/asthma_statistics.stm.
   23. This data came out in the IPCC's *Fourth Assessment Report: Climate Change 2007.* See http://www.ipcc.ch/ipccreports/ar4-wg1.htm.
   24. *An Inconvenient Truth*, DVD, directed by Davis Guggenheim (Hollywood, CA: Paramount, 2007).
   25. US Department of Energy, "China Now Leads in Total Carbon Dioxide Emissions, Says Report," June 27, 2007, http://apps1.eere.energy.gov/news/news_detail.cfm/news_id=11068.
   26. *Associated Press*, "Sea Level Rise Could Flood Many Cities," September 22, 2007, http://news.aol.com/story/_a/sea-level-rise-could-flood-many-cities/20070922130009990001.
   27. Jonathan Overpeck (speech, The University of Arizona, 2009), http://www.youtube.com/watch?v=aCVfQ-_MQXc.
   28. Department of Geosciences Environmental Studies Laboratory, "Climate Change and Sea Level," March 28, 2006, http://www.geo.arizona.edu/dgesl/research/other/climate_change_and_sea_level/sea_level_rise/sea_level_rise_old.htm.
   29. Gore, *An Inconvenient Truth*, 102.
   30. Edward O. Wilson, *The Future of Life* (New York: Vintage Books, 2002), 39.
   31. Gore, *An Inconvenient Truth*, 290–296.

Chapter 3: The Rise of Eco-Capitalism

1. Chris Vogel, "Blowin' in the Wind," *Dallas Observer*, March 26–April 1, 2009, 17.
   2. Anna Clark, "T. Boone Pickens' Roadmap for Green Entrepreneurs," Greenbiz.com, June 1, 2009, http://greenbiz.com/blog/2009/06/01/t-boone-pickens-roadmap-green-entrepreneurs.
   3. Eoin O'Carroll, "Does Wind Power Really Provide More Jobs than Coal?" *Christian Science Monitor*, January 31, 2009, http://features.csmonitor.com/environment/2009/01/31/does-wind-power-really-provide-more-jobs-than-coal.
   4. Kevin Doyle, "Wind Power Industry Hiring in Huge Numbers," *Grist*, July 30, 2008, http://www.grist.org/article/remake-a-living-the-jobs-my-friend-are-blowin-in-the-wind.
   5. Unless otherwise noted, quotes in the text are taken from personal interviews with the author.
   6. Terry Hood, "Wind Energy: Oklahoma's Big Windfall?" Newson6.com, November 10, 2008, http://www.newson6.com/global/story.asp?s=9323126.
   7. "California Governor Schwarzenegger's Green Challenge," California Solar Installation, December 21, 2008, http://californiasolarinstallation.com/archives/tag/schwarzenegger.

8. Colorado Energy News, "Ritter Tops List as Nation's 'Greenest' Governor," July 1, 2009, http://coloradoenergynews.com/2009/07/ritter-tops-list-as-nations-greenest-governor.

9. Office of the Governor, "Governor Schwarzenegger Announces California Green Jobs Corp Funding Recipients," June 29, 2009, http://gov.ca.gov/press-release/12606.

10. Office of the Governor, "Schwarzenegger Signs Legislation to Complete Million Solar Roofs Plan," August 21, 2006, http://gov.ca.gov/index.php?/press-release/3588.

11. Office of the Governor, "Governor Schwarzenegger Praises the Success of California Solar Initiative," June 30, 2009, http://gov.ca.gov/press-release/12609.

12. Cleantech Group, "Clean Technology Venture Investment Reaches Record $8.4 Billion in 2008 Despite Credit Crisis and Broadening Recession," January 6, 2009, http://cleantech.com/about/pressreleases/010609.cfm.

13. Cleantech Group, "Cleantech Index (CTIUS) Rises 16.6% in First Half of 2009," July 16, 2009, http://cleantech.com/about/pressreleases/20090717.cfm.

14. Doris De Guzman, "Cleantech Investments to Slow in 2009," Green Chemicals, January 9, 2009, http://www.icis.com/blogs/green-chemicals/2009/01/cleantech-investments-to-slow.html.

15. Sara Lozanova, "Five Top Countries for Renewable Energy Investment," Triplepundit.com, September 9, 2008, http://www.triplepundit.com/2008/09/5-top-countries-for-renewable-energy-investment.

16. TieTek, "Testimonials," http://www.tietek.com/testimonials.php.

17. Lee Scott, "Twenty-First-Century Leadership" (speech, October 24, 2005).

Chapter 4: God's Green Soldiers

1. J. Matthew Sleeth, *Serve God, Save the Planet* (Grand Rapids: Zondervan, 2007), 3–4.

2. Ibid., 9.

3. Ibid., 4.

4. *The Green Bible*, I-65.

5. Ibid., I-67.

6. Brian D. McLaren, *Everything Must Change: Jesus, Global Crisis, and a Revolution of Hope* (Nashville: Thomas Nelson, 2007), 3.

7. Ibid.

Chapter 5: A Starter's Guide to Greener Living

1. Misty M. Lees, "Put Your Life on a Diet," *Natural Home*, January/February 2005, http://www.naturalhomemagazine.com/Inspiration/2005-01-01/Less-Is-More-Really.aspx?utm_source=iPost&utm_medium=email.

2. "Compact Fluorescent Light Bulbs," Energy Star, http://www.energystar.gov/index.cfm?c=cfls.pr_cfls.

3. Elizabeth Rogers and Thomas M. Kostigen, *The Green Book* (New York: Three Rivers Press, 2007), 5.

4. Ibid., 7.

5. Ibid., 37.

6. Ibid., 38.

7. Science Daily, "'Vampire' Appliances—They Suck Electricity Even When Switched Off—Cost Consumers $3 Billion a Year, Says Cornell Energy Expert," *Science Daily*, September 27, 2002, http://www.sciencedaily.com/releases/2002 /09/020926065912.htm.

8. Daisy Chan, "10 Things Your Dry Cleaner Won't Tell You," *Smart Money*, February 11, 2003, http://www.smartmoney.com/spending/deals/10-things-your-dry-cleaner-wont-tell-you-13908.

9. Rogers and Kostigen, *The Green Book*, 66.

10. Matthew Pryor, "Does Buying in Bulk *Really* Save You Money?" Sound Mind Investing, March 2006, http://www.soundmindinvesting.com/visitor/2006/mar/level1.htm.

11. Kerry Hannon, "'Go Green' Shows How to Save the Earth and Some Dough," *USA Today*, April 11, 2008, http://www.usatoday.com/money/books/reviews/2008-04-06-go-green-live-rich_N.htm.

12. Bill Marsh, "The Battle between the Bottle and the Faucet," *New York Times*, July 15, 2007, http://www.nytimes.com/2007/07/15/weekinreview/15marsh.html?ex= 1342152000&en=dafef28e4ef1fdab&ei=5088&partner=rssnyt&emc=rss.

13. Fuel economy tips are from www.fueleconomy.gov. Cost savings are based on an assumed fuel price of $1.84/gallon. The higher gasoline prices rise, the more savings you can achieve through responsible driving.

14. David Bach, *Go Green, Live Rich* (New York: Broadway, 2008), 7.

15. Eric Schlosser, *Fast Food Nation* (New York: Harper Perennial, 2009), 3.

16. Beatrice Trum Hunter, "Minimizing Food Waste," *Consumer's Research*, April 1, 1998, http://www.highbeam.com/doc/1G1-20652671.html.

17. Bach, *Go Green, Live Rich*, 7.

18. Ibid., 20.

19. Ibid., 56.

20. Ibid., 120.

21. Paul Hawken, Amory Lovins, and L. Hunter Lovins, *Natural Capitalism* (Boston: Little, Brown, 1999), 50.

22. The Center for the New American Dream, "The New American Dream," http://www.newdream.org/about/principles.php.

Chapter 6: Organic Cuisine, Sustainable Wine, and Local Flavor

1. Heather Schoonover and Mark Muller, "Food without Thought: How US Farm Policy Contributes to Obesity," Institute for Agriculture and Trade Policy, November 2006, 65.

2. Cheryl Long and Tabitha Alterman, "Meet Real Free-Range Eggs," *Mother Earth News*, October/November 2007, http://www.motherearthnews.com/Real-Food/2007-10-01/Tests-Reveal-Healthier-Eggs.aspx.

3. Zoe Bradbury, "Organic, Local and Everything Else: Finding Your Way through the Modern Food Fray," *Discussion Course on Menu for the Future* (Portland: Northwest Earth Institute, 2008), 13.

4. John Robbins and Jia Patton, *May All Be Fed* (New York: Avon Books, 1992), 35.

5. James E. Horne and Maura McDermott, *The Next Green Revolution* (New York: The Haworth Press, 2001), 11–17.

6. National Geographic, *The Green Guide*, 31.

7. Ibid., 26.

8. Pryor, "Does Buying in Bulk *Really* Save You Money?"

9. National Geographic, *The Green Guide* (Washington DC: National Geographic Society, 2008), 18; Diane MacEachern, *Big Green Purse* (New York: Avery, 2008), 30–33.

10. Contact vineyards to find distributors of their wines to stores and restaurants in your area.

11. Anna Clark, "Green Wineries Embrace Innovation from the Fields to the Bottle," Greenbiz.com, July 27, 2009, http://www.greenbiz.com/blog/2009/07/27/green-wineries-embrace-innovation-fields-bottle.

Chapter 7: Eco-Chic Cars, Clothes, and Other Essentials

1. The gross domestic product (GDP) is the measure of the size of the national economy. It is the sum of personal consumption, investments, government spending, and net exports. At 70 percent, personal consumption is the largest component of GDP. For more information, see http://www.hoover.org/research/factsonpolicy/facts/4931661.html.

2. William McDonough and Michael Braungart, *Cradle to Cradle* (New York: North Point Press, 2002), 90.

3. William McDonough, quoted in Jenny Lynn Zappala, "Hyper-Green Products Go 'Cradle to Cradle,'" MSNBC, October 12, 2007, http://www.msnbc.msn.com/id/21227970.

4. Prices and figures represent the most accurate data available at time of print. Also, while regular cars get better mileage on the highway than in the city, this is not always the case with hybrids. Driving styles and varying systems play a part in city/highway mileage.

5. James R. Healey, "Test Drive: 2010 Ford Fusion Is Best Gas-Electric Hybrid Yet," August 21, 2009, http://www.usatoday.com/money/autos/reviews/healey/2009-02-05-2010-ford-fusion-hybrid_N.htm.

6. *US News & World Report*, "Ford Fusion Hybrid—What the Auto Press Says," September 8, 2009, http://usnews.rankingsandreviews.com/cars-trucks/Ford_Fusion-Hybrid.

Chapter 8: A Buyer's Guide to Toxin-Free Living

1. Colborn, Dumanoski, and Myers, *Our Stolen Future*, 9.

2. Ibid., 29–36.

3. Ibid., 169.

4. MacEachern, *Big Green Purse*, 46.

5. Environmental Working Group's Skin Deep Cosmetic Safety Database, "Exposures Add Up—Survey Results," June 2004, http://www.cosmeticsdatabase.com/research/exposures.php.

6. Colborn, Dumanoski, and Myers, *Our Stolen Future*, 40.

7. Theo Colborn, "A Controversial Scientist Speaks on Plastics, IQ, and the Womb," *Mother Jones*, March/April 1998, http://www.motherjones.com/politics/1998/03/theo-colborn.

8. National Geographic, *The Green Guide*, 169.

9. MacEachern, *Big Green Purse*, 61–64.

10. Centers for Disease Control and Prevention, *National Report on Human Exposure to Environmental Chemicals* (Atlanta: Centers for Disease Control, 2005), cdc.gov/exposurereport/report.htm.

11. "An Introduction to Indoor Air Quality," US Environmental Protection Agency, January 6, 2009, http://epa.gov/iaq/voc.html.

12. Amy Linn, "An Interview with Green Pediatrician Alan Greene," *Grist*, September 24, 2007, http://www.grist.org/article/greene.

13. Ibid.

14. Sloan Barnett, *Green Goes with Everything* (New York: Atria Books, 2008), 1–2.

15. Nancy and Jim Chuda, "Our Story," Healthy Child, Healthy World, 2008, http://healthychild.org/about/our_story.

16. Ibid.

17. Bach, *Go Green, Live Rich*, 71.

18. National Geographic, *The Green Guide*, 73.

Chapter 10: Urban Oasis or Sustainable Suburb?

1. Rod Dreher, *Crunchy Cons* (New York: Three Rivers Press, 2006), 104.

2. Bryan Walsh, "Recycling the Suburbs," *Time*, March 12, 2009, 48.

3. Laurel Kallenbach, "Cultivating Community," *Natural Home*, March/April 2009, 61–62.

Chapter 11: Green Games Your Kids Will Love

1. Marian Burros, "Obamas to Plant Vegetable Garden at White House," *New York Times*, March 19, 2009, http://www.nytimes.com/2009/03/20/dining/20garden.html.

Chapter 12: Green at Work

1. Anna Clark, "How to Create Change in a Conservative Culture," Greenbiz.com, November 30, 2008, http://www.greenbiz.com/news/2008/11/30/how-create-change-conservative-culture.

2. SustainLane.com, "Four Tips for Breaking into the Job Market," March 2, 2009, http://www.sustainlane.com/reviews/four-tips-for-breaking-into-the-green-job-market/TVVBCCSL7QRTOIKFQQ7X1PQUFDN8.

Chapter 13: Finding Your Voice

1. Eric Carle, *The Very Hungry Caterpillar* (New York: Penguin, 1986), 2.

Anna Clark is president of EarthPeople, a consulting and communications firm that helps clients of all sizes bolster their brands through profitable green strategies. Having begun her career as a knowledge management consultant for PricewaterhouseCoopers and IBM, Anna presently conducts branding and PR campaigns for companies in the clean technology arena.

In addition to her work in green business, Anna writes and speaks on topics ranging from corporate sustainability to creation care. She is the author of the popular Eco-Leadership series for Greenbiz.com and a featured blogger for Sustain-Lane.com. She has been interviewed by media outlets such as *USA Today*, FOX Business News, and Entrepreneur Radio. *Green, American Style* is her first book.

Anna is a member of the Greenbiz Intelligence Panel and the Environmental Forum for the Dallas Institute of Humanities and Culture. She lives in Dallas with her husband Michael and their two children, in one of the first residences in Texas to earn a platinum LEED-certified rating from the US Green Building Council. For more about the author, visit www.annamclark.com.

A Note from the Author

Anna Clark is donating a portion of her royalties from the sales of *Green, American Style* to Feed The Children. This Christian, international, nonprofit relief organization delivers food, medicine, clothing, and other necessities to individuals, children, and families who lack these essentials due to famine, war, poverty, or natural disaster. Visit their website at www.feedthechildren.org.

FEED THE
CHILDREN ®